THINK
LIKE A
SHRINK

100 Principles for Seeing Deeply into Yourself and Others

Emanuel H. Rosen, M.D.
with Tershia d'Elgin

A Fireside Book
Published by Simon & Schuster
New York   London   Toronto   Sydney   Singapore

FIRESIDE
Rockefeller Center
1230 Avenue of the Americas
New York, NY 10020

Fireside and colophon are registered trademarks
of Simon & Schuster Inc.

Designed by William P. Ruoto

Manufactured in the United States of America

10   9   8   7   6   5   4   3   2   1

Library of Congress Cataloging-in-Publication Data

Rosen, Emanuel.
    Think like a shrink : 100 principles for seeing deeply into
yourself and others / Emanuel Rosen ; with Tershia d'Elgin.
        p. cm.
    Includes bibliographical references.
    I. Mental health. I. d'Elgin, Tershia. II. Title.

RA790.R554 2001
616.89—dc21   00-067680

ISBN 0-684-86603-X

In memory of my father,
Joseph D. Rosen, M.D.

ACKNOWLEDGMENTS

By no means can I call this book my own. I owe its contents to so many people that it is impossible to credit them all, though I have made an earnest effort to acknowledge those whose generosity and influence were most profound. I apologize, in advance, to anyone I may have inadvertently omitted.

Above all, I would like to thank Dr. Cal Colarusso, whom I consider a mentor figure in both my personal and professional endeavors. Whatever is right about this book, I owe for the most part to him. At its best, this work reflects his considerable wisdom.

Dr. Glen O. Gabbard inspired me in many ways. As a teacher, he captivated the residents at the Menninger Foundation with his clarity and dedication to instruction. He selflessly reviewed an early version of the manuscript. His book *Psychodynamic Psychiatry* was of immense help in providing me with the background for the personality principles. I am sure that there is much from him that permeates the text, in its better respects.

I am grateful to Dr. Arthur Terr for extensively reviewing early versions of the manuscript over a period of many years and constantly pushing for improvements.

Dr. Constance Dalenberg's talent completely awes me. In a brief time, she was crucial in helping to put into words the very heart and core of what I was trying to communicate. She also unflinchingly reviewed the manuscript for accuracy.

Acknowledgments

I must also thank Dr. Herbert Spohn, Dr. Robert Neveln, and Dr. Sonya Hintz, whose reviews of an early version of the manuscript provided valuable insight into improving it.

My agent, Julie Castiglia, recognized the popular pulse the book needed. Her frank criticism and persuasion escorted the project forward to publication.

I am also grateful to my editor, Caroline Sutton, for recognizing the potential for popular merit of the principle format and for her expertise.

Finally, I thank Hara Estroff Marano at *Psychology Today*, who took a chance on an unknown late-night caller and gave my work the exposure that made this book possible.

CONTENTS

Contents

Contents

Contents

Contents

INTRODUCTION

I come from a family of psychiatrists. At home, thinking like a shrink was second nature. Hence, it wasn't until I myself was in the psychiatrist's chair that the distinction between therapists and the nonpsychiatric community really hit me. They *think* differently! Even though America is inundated with information about explanations for why we feel and act as we do, there is still a dramatic gulf between caring about psychology and thinking as a psychiatrist does. And now, after years in practice, I have come to feel that that gulf is entirely unnecessary, that if more people could think like a shrink the world would be a kinder, more fulfilling place. That conviction inspired me to write this book.

Simply put, shrink-think has one core distinction from everyday thinking: its aptitude for seeing beyond people's actions or words to the underlying defenses that trigger and support them. For shrinks, contact with anyone always elicits a rapid and almost involuntary subtext that suggests plausible reasons for why that person is behaving thus. Knowing that personalities are formed not chosen allows us to perceive even the most difficult people in a broader, less judgmental way.

Cultivating a knack for seeing deeply into people and into oneself is invaluable. In psychotherapy, I have found that it is sometimes beneficial to explain to patients how and why they are doing what they do. This explanation can catalyze change and speed up the therapeutic process. Knowing that these revelations work from firsthand experience, I felt not just patients but the general public might benefit from this knowledge.

Most of us have holes in our awareness. How could I offer the tools to augment that awareness to the widest possible audience? I sat down to create a format for the book that would be informational and fun. It was also important that the material provide solutions as frequently as possible.

Psychiatry is a cumbersome subject, with vast reservoirs of data and opinion as well as frequent controversy. Most self-help books, therefore, address a single aspect of psychiatry such as depression, anxiety, self-esteem, relationships, etc. By contrast, I wanted to offer the reader a way of thinking that transcended the specifics, in part because the specifics are, though important, so infinitely variable, and also because the aspects bear on each other. I reasoned that if I could teach readers how to find relevant psychological themes in their own and others' lives, rather than trying to apply effective remedies to thousands of unseen "patients," I could empower them. Like the old cliché, I wanted to teach people how to fish rather than handing them today's meal.

Finally, I have reduced psychology's basic tenets into psychodynamic principles. The number is arbitrary, for certainly I could not include everything. My objective is to get a "primer" into the hands of the reading public, not cram this very complex field into a crash course. My amalgamation of observations, tips, and insights will alert readers to aspects of their own psyche and to the inner workings of those around them. A glossary at the end defines those terms people hear and use constantly, sometimes without knowing their exact meaning. I have conceived the principles as guideposts; the path they identify leads to *emotional health*.

Emotional health is an individual matter and difficult to define. But I believe Freud's description is still comprehensive: *For someone to be emotionally healthy, they should be able to work and to love.* By *work* he meant productivity in a structured activity, and by *love* he included emotional and sexual demonstrations of affection.

I have tried to write the kind of book that you can open on any page and find insights about your emotional health, and that of others. But psychology is a circuitous and overlapping study, perhaps more than any other field, with every path leading necessarily to another and each destination introducing new points of departure. For this reason, the principle groupings are entirely arbitrary. They are there for the benefit of those who want quick access to a particular subject. That said, I encourage readers to explore other areas. You will be amazed at the influence of issues you may have imagined were irrelevant.

Exploring any of the principles then relating them to your own life should help you to see more deeply into people. In looking at these examples of distorted personality styles, you will see yourself, your family, your friends, and your associates. You'll find yourself, gradually at first, appreciating people beyond the images they portray socially. You will also begin to observe them in terms of their profound struggles. Bit by bit, and with practice, you'll be "thinking like a shrink."

I hope my book will allow people to discover their own insights about themselves when they don't require formal therapy. I also hope that it will leave them more receptive to psychotherapy if they do need it. If I have done my job, my colleagues may agree that by speaking directly to our patients about the principles we usually reserve for our professional discussions, there will be wider acceptance of certain core psychological truths.

Together these objectives comprise my aim—to encourage a more intelligent consumer of mental health information.

THE BIG PICTURE

A Human Is a Human Is a Human

Bill Gates and an Aborigine have a lot in common. They may not hanker after the same clothes, but we can be sure that their primal desires are identical. They both want sustenance. They both want sexual gratification. They both want security. They both want respect. And they both want love.

So what if one may flaunt khakis and the other a loincloth? Irrelevant, a mere expression of cultural bias. Social mores, spiritual beliefs, and priorities vary from culture to culture, and even within the same countries, depending on upbringing and peer expectation. Even in our melting pot of a country, we see great differences in expression and lifestyle between people of different backgrounds and generations.

Nonetheless, distilled down, these discrepancies are but different expressions of the same primal tendencies, hard wired into our genes for the grander purpose of survival, and bearing greatly on our emotional health. You may believe that your son, your daughter, your father, your employer, and so forth are nothing like you. But look deeper. You'll see that though the methods may be different, the needs are the same. Recognizing common needs is a first step toward cultivating more tolerant attitudes about differences, and happily, in terms of therapy, this commonality broadens human understanding.

Fantasies Rule

As often as we are all admonished to get a grip on reality, the echo of desire irrepressibly jars, shaking the foundation right out from under real life. And why not? Reality is so much more difficult to control than a confection over which we, and we alone, have total creative tyranny. Fantasy makes a great retreat, or if not "great," at least familiar.

Everyone has fantasies. These can be trivial or all-encompassing. Either way, the greater the distance between the fantasy and the reality, the more arduous the psychological task. A shrink or loved one can only help a deluded patient accept reality *mentally*. However, no one, no how, can excise the emotional longing that fuels and will continue to fuel escapist tendencies. The most skillful therapists help to narrow the chasm between the perceived want and achievable goals, and often it is the former that needs the most attention.

All fantasies have a source. With encouragement, day-trippers will sometimes reveal the associations they make with their fantasies. A man who would take six women to bed at once might want to feel more manly. Or the woman whose desire is a 10,000-square-foot chateau complete with turrets may have an exaggerated need for security. Find out *why* they evoke those fantasies and you'll be learning what makes them tick.

Fantasies can be so vivid that if an event shatters one, it can precipitate an emotional crisis, even if the individual is unaware or only dimly aware of its existence. In the case of a fear-based fantasy, for example, a person might get severely depressed on entering law school or on getting married before their older sibling if he or she has the unconscious fantasy that besting the sibling will lead to annihilation. But a fantasy meltdown may eventually lead sufferers to grounding their ideas in reality.

Identifying the anxiety at the source of the fantasy—which usually has its origin in childhood—is a first step toward mitigating its influence. Based on a more thorough understanding of why they fantasize, dreamers can design more achievable goals. Small steps, taken incrementally, will lead them to more satisfying lives. They may even reach to achieve their pie in the sky, instead of just thinking about it.

The Unconscious Mind
Is a Constant, Invisible Influence

It's not that there is no free will. But there is too often un-recognized forces guiding our reactions, both inconsequential and life-altering.

I once argued with my late psychiatrist father, "The very word *unconscious* suggests that we are unaware of it, and there-fore it does not matter."

He replied simply, "Some are more unaware of it than others."

It is just this lack of awareness that makes us emotionally stupid.

As actors and actresses in our own private play, only infre-quently do we recognize that our unconscious is subtly yanking the strings. We do this, we do that, all the while imagining that we are just acting spontaneously to what life serves up. The more neurotic we are, the less awareness we have of what the script actually says, of how much of our circumstances are due to our unconscious. Without awareness, we get stuck in patterns that become painfully familiar, but that we nevertheless repeat over and again.

Eventually, the unconscious seems to raise its own alert in the form of emotional suffering. Frequent overblown reactions are a sign. Repeated painful outcomes that run against con-scious intent are another. The unconscious is trying to become more conscious!

By profession, shrinks commit to the healing power of "increased awareness," but it is slow going. Anyone's insight regarding his or her unconscious only begins the therapeutic process. It is like acquiring a brand-new sense in tiny increments. Imagine the fog of unawareness thinning slightly. The freshly conscious person sees the dim outline of an unknown shape (which is actually their own thought process). Just then the fog thickens again, and not until it clears for a second time will the glimmer reoccur. And so forth.

Even more difficult and requiring months and sometimes years of practice is the glacial "working through" phase that will make hitherto unconscious patterns conscious, then gradually transform choices into more nourishing ones.

Sociopathy Is Common

People are just naturally duplicitous, often without knowing it. They cultivate personas that mask their cravings, frequently so thoroughly that they themselves do not know what nasty deeds they are capable of until they perform them. Even then, they can fall back on the survival instincts they have relied upon since childhood, veiling or abjuring the full-fledged depravity of which they are the author. Unless they are caught or otherwise come a cropper, their damaging schema may continue and escalate.

Since turpitude is everywhere, it is important to reserve trust early in relationships. Sociopaths come in all guises and their true colors may not show immediately. Even the sweetest, most seemingly generous people may eventually bring out an agenda that reveals an utter lack of scruples.

Likewise, since you are just as inclined to encounter sociopathy as not, don't be shocked when it emerges. Still your mind. Keeping steady in the face of what may appear to be reckless disingenuousness will allow you to take in all the facts. And it will help keep the fallout from whatever chaos the sociopath has prompted, as it affects you, to a minimum. Sometimes, your stillness may even inadvertently serve to protect others if, by not being confronted critically, the sociopath finds his or her way to healing.

It is human to be judgmental rather than dispassionate and scientific. And it is very difficult to inhibit the natural distaste for dishonorable acts, particularly when they come as a surprise. However, judgment personalizes what may have been an event that has nothing whatsoever to do with you. Judgment always clouds observance of the sociopath's underlying issues. And these may be the very problems that undermined his or her moral responsibility to begin with. Repugnance will limit your empathy, and without empathy and patience you will never be able to guide another person toward healing.

You Can't Choose Your Feelings

Hearts are like wind. Though they may be diverted, they cannot be stopped. Altering the way we *think* about people, events, and issues is one matter. But trying to change the way we *feel* about them is almost impossible. As the French philosopher Blaise Pascal wrote, "The heart has it reasons which reason knows not of."

Try as we might, a struggle to overcome feelings cannot be waged. Regret them. Berate them. Stanch and deny them. They are still there. In fact, trying to eliminate them seems to redouble their influence and can stymie emotional progress. Ironically, the more people defend against their unwanted feelings, the more they drive away the resources available to overcome them. Feelings—negative or positive—"just are." The conversation with oneself about why one shouldn't feel, on the one hand, annoyance, hostility, or hatred, or on the other hand, inappropriate or unreciprocated lust or love (these are examples) tends to reinforce the feelings rather than mitigate them.

Though you cannot choose your feelings, you can choose your *thinking about the feelings*. The change in thinking is the action that alleviates the tension and may ultimately allow you to master, however indirectly, the feelings themselves.

My advice is to throw the doors open and let those ill-favored feelings loose, complete with tears and curses and rage, no matter how "unreasonable." It is far more productive just to accept them. Go ahead and indulge. This usually brings about a near-mystical transformation.

First, you will be amazed at the relief you experience. And on its heels, very likely, will be a sense of moving beyond what you have been trying to avoid. It's remarkable how catalyzing choosing to *change the way you think about your feelings* is. Your heart will be free, free for another episode of feeling!

In Order to Comprehend More Clearly, Stand Back

Most of us are too close to our personal problems to see them accurately. With our consciousness pressed against them, we only focus on details. Often these details, and our emotions about them, blind us to the big picture. By locking tightly onto these aspects like a fanged dog, we may overlook other approaches to the problem and other ways of appreciating that reality.

It isn't easy to see problems, much less fix them, when we are enmeshed in them. However, it may be that letting go of a narrow perception will, in and of itself, present solutions or perhaps even solve the problem. For example, imagine that your perspective is that someone else is overly sensitive. That other person continually accuses you of being boorish. Does one of you have to be wrong to make the other right? Not necessarily. Suppose you slap your friend on the back, unaware of his sunburn. He snaps at you. Was he overreacting? No. Your action and his can only be understood as a unit. The "truth" of an interaction is usually within the interaction.

There are some circumstances that you can improve and others that no amount of tenacious pursuit will rectify. This principle is so important that Alcoholics Anonymous and other recovery programs use it as a fundamental idea. In their Serenity Prayer they beseech God to help them change the things they can, accept the things they can't change, and cultivate the wisdom to know the difference. Good advice.

Issues or relationships that become fixations, that are preoccupying to a paralyzing extent, are exactly those anxieties that need to be relaxed. Imagine if your mind were a galloping horse and the fixations rough terrain. Your inclination would be to stiffen. This tautness, however, does not smooth the journey, either for the horse or the mind. Let go. Find your mind's rhythm. Rock with it.

FAMILY INFLUENCES

Our Families Are *Always* with Us, *Forever* . . .

It all goes back to the original litter that included you and your siblings, overseen by your parents. The patterns of activity in the familial dog pile make their mark and shape each of us as a friend, coworker, and partner for a lifetime. In psychoanalytical terms, this is called object relations, a bland way of saying that we all lug our families around in our heads forever.

Every one of us has the tendency to assume our puppy roles or those of our parents. Whether we regard these roles as stellar is neither here nor there. Unconscious habit will win out over conscious good intentions.

As an example, for people who were teased a lot as children, mockery may seem like a good way to express intimacy. If beloved elders extracted curtsies, bows, and silence before they would acknowledge our worthiness, we will likely equate love with subservience. People who come from argumentative households gravitate toward knockdown dragouts in their personal and professional relationships. Same goes for criticism. Affectionate families produce affectionate children. And so forth.

Though unconscious, it is not coincidental that people find themselves inveigled by scenarios that have much in common with the sitcom or drama in which they grew up. A coworker frustrates you in the same way that your brother does. You befriend a woman and later realize she reminds you of your mother, etc. This is as true of rewarding relationships as it is of destructive ones. Even if you try to restrain yourself, you still find yourself acting like a new edition of one of your parents, usually your same-sex parent. And you are pulled, as if by tractor beam, to partners who remind you of your opposite-sex parent. We spend our lives churning out new generations of the people we grew up with, inadvertently cloning our friendships, personalities, and marriages after them. The dialog is the same. The conflicts are familiar. The resolutions get resolved or stay unresolved in exactly the same way.

It's that devilish "object relations" at work. If your most intimate interactions seem like an episode you don't want to relive, your object relations may need some overhaul.

. . . And What We Know of Intimacy, We Learned from Mom and Dad

This principle is an extension of the previous one about object relations. As children we all learned how intimacy "acts" by watching the "pros"—our parents. If Mom was a master of the inflicted guilt trip, we may have grown up believing that making a partner feel guilty is an integral part of showing affection. If Dad put all kinds of conditions on his acceptance of Mom, that laying down of expectations may seem like the best accompaniment to a kiss. If either parent treated the other as an inferior, a situation that includes cowering may seem as natural as romance. It's not that people don't know they are being obnoxious when they behave thus; it just feels right because that's the way their parents acted.

As we mature, we may unconsciously revert to these defective expressions of love. And often we are attracted to people who act as a loved one acted. The most potentially lurid situation of all occurs when both syndromes dovetail. That complicates the love recipe even more.

Qualities we really love initially, such as someone's naïveté and lack of materialism, may later become immensely irritating when the spouse neglects to pay the gas bill on time. Or a lover's easy manner of getting things done seems tyrannical once we are sharing a roof with her or him. This is because we have assumed what's called our reciprocal roles. No longer on the loose, our spouse-self has emerged, a younger replica of the parent we may have vowed we'd never be.

Albeit unconscious, it is not by chance that our mates react to us in ways that seem to have less to do with us than with their parents. When this is destructive, as it often is, it is important to get to the heart of our heartfelt connections, overcoming or working through these preconceptions we cannot seem to discard. This takes a lot of self-examination and patience, for both partners.

Much of Self-Esteem Comes from
Mothers' Nurturing

Stable, healthy mothering can buffer against a tremendous amount of pathology from other family members, from peers, and from life itself. This mothering person need not be a mother, of course, but can also be any other *primary* caregiver. Here is why: Loving mothers get *internalized.* The memory of their warm words and deeds buttresses us—from the inside out—with a feeling of being safe and on course.

By contrast, a mommy dearest who fails to safeguard us against predation and turmoil seeds us with a very different self-image, all the lower if her nonchalant care also included harsh criticism. We are more likely to feel vulnerable and unlovable and bad throughout life. We perceive ourselves as wronged because our childhood experience taught us to expect to be wronged.

The flip side of this principle is that one cannot upgrade self-esteem by force. No small number of encounter groups or self-help books can revolutionize Mom. Her inadequacy is in there for good. Frequently, self-esteem is so deeply cemented in the personality that the best one can accomplish is to master techniques for dealing with anxiety and conflict. Among these techniques are the following: First, remember that avoiding anxiety issues only makes them worse. Keep in mind that you have the right to be *respected.* Remind yourself of past successes. Lean on your "cheerleaders," as people who have your best interests at heart, to support your big decisions.

Those Who Don't Remember Their Childhood
May Want to Forget It

Superficially stable types sometimes draw a complete blank on their upbringing. Whenever someone mentions the salad days, they briskly change the subject. They don't even have the desire to retrieve their childhood memories. Unless and until life events force these individuals into introspection, they continue on, without a backward glance, seemingly without a yesterday. Others may at times envy their apparent sangfroid, if they, like most people, remember their own childhood all too well.

Childhood can be an important passage to recollect because that is where our scripts are written. Those great casting directors—our genes and our families—cast us in the role we will play in life. People who remember their childhood are ahead of the game, even if they received a crummy role. The memories may be like those of a long, drawn-out, head-on collision, but at least they can grasp what made them what they are. And that awareness allows them, when need be, to alter the script as adults, albeit with effort and perseverance. On the course to emotional health, that puts them far ahead of those who must repress childhood memories, whose resistance to revisiting their early years prevents them from redressing the damage.

Sometimes, people can get through a whole lifetime without revisiting their childhood, though rarely. Forgotten memories may resurface in close relationships or with a therapist or frequently even at random. Intimate conversations unlock the coffer and dislodge the recollections; that's what makes them intimate. Then, together, friends or lovers, or patients and therapists, can flush out the flawed casting, examine what went awry, and rewrite the script for a future more worth living.

The Ills of the Fathers, or Mothers, Really Are Visited upon the Children

This paraphrased quotation from the Bible is manifest in our communities. For whatever reason, whether "nature" or "nurture," some children and adults really seem to be wired for violence, and the tendency is passed through the family. Without thinking first, they act impulsively and aggressively. A violent psychopath cannot get in touch with his or her conscience, and mundane events cannot provide adequate distance from the inner void; but the adrenaline rush of brutality does.

Children who are either unloved or fail to perceive love grow up caring only about themselves. As they go through life, they project the lovelessness on everyone they meet. Experiencing no affection coming toward them, they automatically assume other people are bad. Nowhere do they see trust. Nowhere do they see rules that make sense to them. Nowhere do they find someone from whom they will accept authority or even collaboration. This is not the type of person one would want to date, marry, or hire. They feel hell-bent on distinguishing themselves from others, on widening the gulf between themselves and the other guy. Since they perceive everyone else as "bad," being different makes them "good."

Psychopaths don't have just a chip or two on their shoulder. They are all chip. Therefore, they can't help but embark on a path of destruction plotted as a sort of retribution. Hurting others adds to their delusion that they are above humankind. Tragically, it gives them the sense of self that they could not extract from their childhoods.

Only if psychopathic tendencies are intercepted during childhood is there a "cure" for the propensities. As they mature, these people become dyed-in-the-wool menaces. Adult-phase psychopaths are very difficult to treat. Many heroic efforts have shown that the best we can do is to monitor them carefully and contain them in institutions such as prisons. This is not true of criminals who demonstrate guilt and/or depression.

Boundaries Define People
the Way Borders Define Countries

When an utter stranger bares his soul, sparing no details, it is a good indicator that he has no regard for boundaries. Beware. Like any colonialist, those who do not honor boundaries may have a paucity of assets within their own borders.

People who cannot figure out where they leave off and other people begin may be victims of childhood incest or they may suffer from mental illness. Having endured invasion and open season on their own privacy, they may be ill-prepared to distinguish their territory from that of others. Quite understandably, they *cannot stop themselves* because they have no real idea of where the demarcation is. And psychological boundaries are often not as easily distinguished as those clearly cordoned off in a visual display.

People who hear voices or hallucinate, paranoids, for example, often cannot help severely disregarding boundaries. Naturally, there are less dramatic examples wherein a momentary lapse causes more emotionally healthy people to cross the line without asking first.

Everybody has need to fortify his or her frontier and make daily decisions about who enters the territory and to what extent. Those who don't know how need encouragement, best given in the form of questions. Generally, this line of inquiry asks the person to distinguish between what is true for him or her and what might have been inadvertently imposed on the other person. For instance, one might ask of the person describing a situation: "Did he actually say that? Or do you think you might be imagining that he would have said that?" "Are you sure that those concerns you feel he has aren't your own concerns?" Or make it personal: "Did I say those words? Or did you project that onto me?"

Psychologists and psychiatrists deal with boundary issues constantly, as patients often try to hang responsibility for their lives on those treating them, and using their techniques may serve in some situations. A good therapist constantly has to psychically cordon off what is personal and what is not, reminding himself or herself, "I care, but it is not my life." Although this sometimes comes off as insensitive, particularly to very needy people, it forces the patient to look within for personal resources.

Successful Neuroses Help People Fail

By adulthood, most of us have developed and refined some pretty elaborate hang-ups. Others may see these hang-ups as self-defeating. But they "work" for the person who contrived them. The key to these so-called coping mechanisms is their *familiarity*. The problem is this: As long as our mad methods reproduce familiar results, we never heal.

Megalomaniacs, for example, may make more money and lord over more people, but they do not necessarily mature emotionally. If an avoidant person succeeds in avoiding commitments, his anxiety decreases, but he does not grow. If an unstable person manages to get someone to take care of her, she will stay unstable. The neuroses remain viable, but the lives are not truly maximized and the underlying pain is never addressed.

Shrinks believe that anxiety in right dosages is the best tonic. Anxiety entreats us to grow. We can choose to say "not now" or even "never!" But there will always be more opportunities, right up into old age. If we accept anxiety's invitation and boldly confront its possibilities, we usually discover that our fears were far disproportionate to the challenge, and we are better people for having tried.

SEX

The Way People Feel About Sex
Is Critical to Their Psychology

Ever since Carl Jung's reluctance to acknowledge sex's centrality distanced him from Sigmund Freud, many therapists have argued that "drive theories" were irrelevant and archaic, but I disagree. Let them try going without sex for three months, and they will rediscover drive theory all over the place.

Like a face with an extra nose, sex is a hard subject to ignore. If sex were not so significant, and our outlook about it ambiguous, it would not be a taboo. We would not go to such great lengths to avoid mentioning it.

Sexual functioning and sexual history reveal a tremendous amount about what people are really like. And though a sticky subject, sex certainly bears the same or greater clout as feelings and cognition in the therapeutic process. It discloses a patient's confidence, fears, aggressions, needs, fantasies, feelings of adequacy and inadequacy, ability to trust, level of compassion, their *everything*.

The reasons that sex is so charged a subject are complex and perhaps, ultimately, beyond quantifying. Suffice it to say that sex is a meeting ground for the body and the conscious, which happens to include one of the deepest primal urges, the urge to reproduce. Also on hand are sentiments about parents, body consciousness, sensuality, and sensitivity. It's too heavy an array to dismiss.

I do not deny that discussion of sex requires more tact, empathy, and care than any other issue. It takes a monumental amount of trust before people will dare to talk freely about sex in more than just casual terms. And even then, it isn't an easy topic to qualify because it is simply so personal. Nevertheless, therapists and people who can gracefully wield this loaded gun know it delivers results.

Whenever Two People of the Same Sex Are in a Room, There Is Always Homosexual Tension, Even If They Are Not Aware of It

Startling news. All people, independent of their sexual preferences, have both heterosexual and homosexual drives, though the homosexual drives may be unconscious, barely conscious, or latent. Heterosexuals repress homosexual drives because these are unwanted or unacceptable, or perhaps because of biology that we have yet to understand fully. Nevertheless, these impulses are evident to anyone who administers long-term analytic therapy.

Those who are wriggling uncomfortably at this bulletin should know that an occasional homosexual impulse does not alone define a sexual orientation. We are each defined by our sexual *behavior,* not mere impulses.

When heterosexuals honor their naturally occurring bisexuality as healthy, they find more tolerance for homosexuals. They also cultivate more freedom in sexual expression with the opposite sex. A lot of what makes good lovers is not sex-specific. For example, men who are able to demonstrate sensuality, sensitivity, and vulnerability—characteristics we associate with the feminine—are superior lovers. Their counterparts, the women who don't shy from aggression and even dominance between the sheets, are also desirable. And importantly, people who are comfortable with both their masculine and feminine drives are more relaxed in the sack. Relaxation is, for most, a prerequisite for the most sumptuous sexual pleasures.

Yes, Children Do Want to be Sexual with Their Opposite-Sex Parents . . .

Oedipus became his mother Jocasta's lover, and Electra did the likewise with her father, Agamemnon. They did it, and most of us haven't. But that doesn't mean it hasn't crossed our minds.

The conscious Oedipal urge need not last a lifetime, but often does occur between the ages of three and six. Children of that age don't really know what sex is, but they do have sexual feelings. They like to touch themselves. They notice the difference between sitting on a parent's lap and jumping rope. Following that stage, children usually set about sublimating their sexual impulses with Mom or with Dad. This peaks as they approach their own sexual maturation. Even the notion of their parents having sex with each other may be too awful to contemplate. The pubescent and adolescent child unconsciously redoubles the effort to bury Oedipus and Electra . . . with a vengeance.

But the longing for mutual expression of sexual love with opposite-sex parents seems impossible to extinguish. Many common relationship problems result from the incomplete repression of this core conflict. Even as adults, we tend to revisit the competitive triangular Mom-Dad-Me relationships with significant others. Our unconscious lust for a parent can even put a damper on intimacy.

Returning to Oedipus himself, young Oedipus became involved with his mother when he ran away from self-knowledge.

The lesson is that acceptance of unpleasant truths protects against disturbing internal tendencies. So arriving at a conscious realization that the triangle exists may dispel the anxiety. Some people must abandon the burdensome task of burying natural urges. There is no conflict. There just "is." Afterward, they can relax more, knowing that their fears are common ones and that they are not alone with them.

I am aware that this principle is misused by pedophiles as a justification and I want to make clear that that is not my intention here.

. . . And Electra and Oedipus
Keep Psychiatrists in Business

Women's competition with other women and men's competition with other men, when excessive, may be an adult extension of children vying with their same-sex parents for the attention of their opposite-sex parents. We shrinks call these fixations unresolved residuals of the Electra complex and Oedipus complex, respectively. If you are a person who doubts your worth as a woman or as a man, and if you are perpetually driven to flaunt your femininity or masculinity, you may be acting out a very common theme named after these mythical screwups.

Electral- and Oedipal-based rivalries often lead patients into liaisons or marriages that have less to do with their trophy partners than with the competitors they have staved off. Likewise, people who shoulder their way into positions of authority for the sheer pleasure of annihilating other contenders often discover unsavory obligations on the other end. Since satisfaction only comes with "getting," they rarely find fulfillment with "having." Off to the shrink they go!

A life devoted to proving one's superiority can be extremely frustrating and painful, not just for the contender but for others around him or her. The only way to slough the complex is to size up your masculinity or femininity truthfully, then accept it. Decide *who* (not what) you want to be, and *get on with it*. Why misspend a whole life showing up for others?

Women Do Not Suffer from Penis Envy
Nearly As Much As Men Do

Only one half of the earth's occupants are susceptible to real penis envy. This affliction, which so dogs some men, is a preoccupation carried over from the Oedipal phase children go through from ages three to six. During that stage kids see everything in terms of magnitude. They are preoccupied by how fast they are, how smart they are, how big their house is, and so forth. *Size matters.* The irony is that, at this age, boys seldom worry about the size of their member.

Not until adolescence, when genitalia suddenly find new purpose, can penis proportions suddenly become a fixation. Locker-room exposure can increase the anxiety, particularly for those with less hefty penises. Even men who are normal size, but insecure, can sweat at the urinal too.

Though a monumental internal issue, penis size is not a popular topic. Hardly any man discusses his little problem, because it is just too embarrassing to bring up. Therefore, the longing for more ample genitalia has the added onus of needing to be secreted.

Thankfully, most women don't assess men by the length and breadth of their family jewels. Women, overall, are often much more concerned with having a sense of security in the relationship. Their own erotic pleasure is usually a close second concern.

Women May Feel That Physical Attractiveness Is a Passage to Security and Fulfillment

While men may hang their self-esteem on something as relatively incidental as their penis size, women tend to go in for full-body envy and overhaul. Since there is no sensible reason why their eligibility should hinge on a flawless body and stylish wardrobe, we can only blame societal influences.

Everyone admires attractive people. However, just as penis size is much more an issue for men than women, men's insistence on 36-24-36 proportions can be exaggerated too, most often by companies wanting to sell women tight jeans, diet foods, exercise programs, and new breasts.

Though body-consciousness is certainly not unique to women, it is much more prevalent among the double X chromosomers.

Sometimes Sex Can Be Used
As a Form of Repayment

In a nonreciprocal relationship, one person provides all the emotional support while the other talks his or her ear off. This sort of one-way neediness can create a power imbalance. So the needy participant may pull out his or her libido, ostensibly using it as currency to demonstrate appreciation. More likely flirtation is a quid pro quo effort to balance the relationship, to take back some of the power. Sex may also serve as an incentive to keep the "advisor" committed to advising. This dynamic occasionally induces unethical psychotherapists onto the couch with their patients.

To the needy person, a calm, attentive confidant who reveals nothing is a tabula rasa. The usual information that directs human conversation and relatedness is missing. This vacuum of data on one side unbalances the relationship. The indefatigable patient (or acquaintance) can merely "fill in the blanks," attributing all kinds of emotions and characteristics to his or her sounding board, usually culling liberally from an imagination that knows no bounds. The more dire the need for a benign figure, the stronger the idealization of the listener. And with idealization, a certain desire can reinforce the urge to use sex as a way to rebalance the exchange. The patient may sexualize the relationship as a defense against other underlying feelings, of vulnerability, for instance.

Paying for treatment with real money keeps the power balance more equitable. It gives the patient clout. Still, it does not often deter the patient's overinvolvement with the *perceived* emotions of the psychotherapist.

When this kind of relationship exists outside of the therapeutic context, there may be no overt conflict since it meets everybody's needs, albeit unhealthy needs. On the other hand, either player may become resentful. Here again, watch out when unhealthy people become healthy.

Genital Potency Does Not Equal Sexual Potency

Reliable, functional sexual machinery is not to be taken for granted. Those who have it can rejoice; those who do not think of little else. But orgasms are not the same as intimacy. Just because everyone *comes* does not mean partners cannot *leave*. And leave they will if sex is merely a demonstration of smoothly operating gear and tackle.

A man, or a woman, can have sex with fifty or a hundred or a thousand people. A reputation of libidinous excellence may even follow. But somewhere along the line, some clear thinker is going to ask, "If that guy or gal is such a great lay, why can't he or she sustain a real connection?"

Underlying feelings of inadequacy may be behind what looks like a pursuit to occupy more bodies. That serial lovers break more hearts may be an unintentional ramification. If you corner a lothario, of either gender, you may get him or her to admit that quantity does not make up for quality . . . and that something significant is missing, despite all the conquests.

This is not to suggest that lustful supercharge means the wiring for intimacy is amiss, because it need not be. Both sides of the circuitry can, ideally, function at full wattage. With combined genital and sexual potency, what is turned on won't turn off.

RELATIONSHIPS

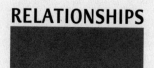

Intimate Relationships Are the *Only* Real Measuring Stick for Emotional Health

We envy a wildly successful tycoon. We admire a gorgeous movie star who is adored worldwide. A major-league pitcher, cheered by fans, seems to "have it all." Even the colleague down the hall appears to be enviably unstoppable. But does professional triumph equal personal victory? Not necessarily. Never confuse success or even confidence with psychological well-being.

Money, charm, and kudos cannot replace quality relationships. Often they screen emotional disturbances, blinding close relatives and everyone else to tremendous unhappiness lurking beneath. Bravado and charisma, however desirable, can also be distancing mechanisms that keep the public, friends, and even family from detecting inner turbulence.

Sometimes these people use their élan as a device for blaming any problems in an intimate relationship on the other partner. Their record of achievement seems to confirm, "Surely, the fault cannot be my own." This failure to own up to their share of the tribulation, while keeping their noses clean, doesn't make them compassionate, reliable, generous, or any of the other qualities that characterize a desirable mate.

So, save your envy until you've weighed the whole picture. Set aside superficial outward characteristics, and look instead at a person's deeper emotional expression by asking four questions: Do they have long-lived and committed intimate relationships? Does excessive conflict occur at or around their work environment? Do they find satisfaction there? Did they get along with their family and do they still?

If an individual seems unapproachable, and lacks genuinely warm relationships with those who should be his or her closest allies, no matter how great the apparent success, there *are* psychological problems.

We Cannot Help
Transferring Relationship Patterns

Does your wife seem like your mom in wife's clothing? Or how about your boss? Does he make you squirm just as your dad did? Imposing previously etched relationship patterns onto current relationships is called transference. We all do it. And we can't help it. We had the patterns hammered into us early on, usually in childhood. As a consequence, we jam new people we meet into the holes left by those earlier impressions. The new "pegs" may be important, such as a spouse or therapist, or trivial, such as a delivery person or clerk. Every encounter comes at us through the overlay of prior relationships. This can't help but bias impressions and put our minds to work on expectations that may or may not pan out.

Hence, the attraction we call chemistry may not be entirely mystical after all. It may be shaped by transference. Most significantly, we may be attracted to people who remind us of our parents. This is true whether our childhood experience was good or bad. If our parents were nurturing, we seek to reinforce them through repetition. If there was childhood turbulence, we seek to resolve the distress through another similar sort of person. For people who are really determined to overcome childhood issues, the slimmest points of parity may be enough to trigger transference. A woman might be attracted, in part, to a man named Joe, just because that was her father's name, for example.

In cases of strong chemistry—that is strong attraction or revulsion based, whether consciously or unconsciously, on earlier memory—it can take a long time and some pain to appreciate the new person for who he or she really is, instead of what you project. This process can be fraught with disappointment as the object of your chemistry emerges as someone different from the person you projected, as is usually the case. Just as often, you can be pleasantly surprised to learn that your dark imaginings are unfounded.

As qualities you did not initially perceive emerge, it can also be tremendously rewarding and even healing. The therapeutic value of deconstructing transference may be in its forced assessment of what is really nurturing and what is just an attempt to extract nurturing from withholding people. Awareness of trust patterns that are uniquely yours allows you to peel back the distorting transparencies. By perceiving people more objectively, you can respond more appropriately.

Aggressive Men Often Cower
Around Their Wives and Girlfriends

A guy who throws his weight around in public like a front-end loader most often cultivates this style in compensation for the circumstances of his childhood, which may have included a ball-busting mother and distant father, and a phenomenon of contrasts can result. Men like this find a way to re-create their boyhood subjugation by seeking out and marrying women who rag on them constantly. When they are around their wives, they turn to jelly. It's stupefying to discover a he-man cringing before someone who seems to have less power. But it happens all the time.

Simply put, the wife becomes a surrogate for his mother. She is an extortionist. She criticizes his shortcomings and "castrates" him either by derogating his lovemaking or by refusing him sexually or both. This combination can result in impotence unless both partners realize that unresolved childhood issues, not love, motivate their behaviors.

Needy People Immediately
Create Chaos in Relationships

When it comes to relationships, unhealthy people can very quickly wreak havoc, committing the full gamut of identifiable psychological transgressions. This rap sheet usually commences with identifiable boundary problems. Having sex with a stranger is a common point of departure. After a few hours, distorted perceptions about what having had sex might mean rush in, bringing their irksome friends, the high expectations. In other words, people who jump out of their clothes before learning last names may also jump to wrong conclusions.

It usually isn't long before unresolved issues with the opposite-sex parent appear in the gathering weather system. And then, in an effort to fulfill their destiny of being eternally rejected, these very needy people may depart on a ricocheting path of compulsive, invasive actions that range from annoying to abusive. There is no telling what they'll do next. They are masters of extemporizing, at their own expense and at others.' Still don't get the picture? Think Glenn Close. Think knives.

Criticism Destroys Relationships

When was the last time someone you were criticizing said, "Gee, thanks"? Even though the most common cause of criticism is disappointment over unmet expectations, criticism still seems like an introduction to spar. It does not feel like it is about solving problems together. Criticism tends to rob relationships of trust. It undermines love and connection.

When a person does something that rankles you, it may be necessary to mention it rather than letting your feelings fester. But you will get a better response if you couch the criticism in positive feedback. This is old wisdom, but we forget because life is competitive and we are in a hurry: Sugar-coated medicine goes down more easily. First tell the offender all the good aspects of what has occurred, then mention the offense, almost as an afterthought. That way he or she will be motivated not to offend again.

It is also important to distinguish between the behavior and the person. As we've all read in parenting and relationship books, *say "me" not "you."* Describe the feeling the person's action stirs up; do not go for the jugular. For example, say, "It hurts me when you ogle other women," versus, "You disgusting pig."

From time to time, it seems convenient to concentrate on others' foibles instead of our own shortcomings, and this may be when criticism occurs. But it's unproductive and unfair to ask the people around us to suffer our misplaced antipathy. This neither corrects the situation nor mitigates our own hurt. It just empties our lives of love. Make sure criticism is merited before you unload it.

Shallow People Rebound Quickly, Too Quickly

"Plug and play" is a perfect approach to romance for people whose emotional demands are no more profound than a puddle. Usually, they are attracted by looks alone. Money may also be a lure. The less they know about the other person, the better. Ideally, the object of their desire would not speak their same language.

Evidently, a relationship with such a character is as rewarding as a drought. One after another, their pitiable lovers or spouses get fed up and bail, with whatever self-confidence and emotional well-being remains to them. To the plug-and-player, the passing parade of his or her love life (if one may call it that) may not fluster them in the least. Since the demands are trivial, they are replaceable.

On the other hand, it may. Even people who only see skin-deep can tire of breaking in new mates, then breaking up. It's expensive. And redundant. As the weeks pass, they'll anticipate then hear the now-familiar lamentations that likely include "you're not in touch with your feelings . . . or mine." Mere tedium over the reiterating cycle that their relationships take can provoke them to seek change.

If it doesn't, life events also have a way of intervening. Only rarely does someone make it all the way through his or her life as a heel. If tedium doesn't fell them, financial problems or physical setbacks eventually impede these people's ability to suck blood from new victims. Having never invested real care in anyone else, they find no care is reciprocated. Hardship may well force them to explore more depth in themselves and more depth in relationships. As a result, and with luck, they will discover the inordinate gift that the depth affords.

Women Who Angle for Male Attention
May Never Have Hooked Maternal Affection . . .

We all know women who draw men like pest strips. They are fun, colorful, eye-catching, and vivacious—the sort that makes men feel special. Many come by their ability to attract male attention naturally, since they may have enjoyed a close relationship with their father—closer, usually, than to their mother.

Women whose mothers never gave them a second thought, for whatever reason, always harbor an unrequited need for female nurturing, conscious or not. Or as shrinks put it, they don't need a penis, they need a breast. Lacking a mommy, they became a daddy's girl. However, this overly intense relationship produced sexual tension. And the only way for a growing daughter to deal with its intensity is to banish sexuality. The result is that daddy's girls may become far less interested in having sex with men than with simply collecting them. Although these women are sexually appealing as adults, and they may even be teases, their admirers should know that sex is not their objective. It's only attention they are after. Sadly, the male attention, no matter how abundant, is never enough to sate them. They cannot compensate for quality with quantity.

Not having known soothing receptive mothering, these beguiling women have no female model of intimacy. If they can befriend other women with a need to mother, this pairing may be a symbiotic match. With a nurturing female relationship to rely upon, they may be freer to explore intimacy with men.

. . . And Don Juan Had an Absent Father

A corollary to the last principle is the man who "loves" women. He doesn't want one intimate partner, or even one woman at a time. He wants them all. This man may have enjoyed a close relationship with his mother but little contact with his father. His parents may have divorced. His father may have moved away or died. Or maybe his father was just unavailable for other reasons. Whatever the circumstances, the boy without a dad matured into a collector of females.

The same sort of sexual tension that feeds the last syndrome feeds this one. Don Juan is unable to act on or overcome his disproportionately large emotional and sexualized connection with his mother. Even as an adult, the son persists in trying to resolve this. He tries it out with as many women as he can ensnare. He cannot settle into one rich relationship because he is still unconsciously cocooned with his mama.

Once Don Juan knows that moving ahead with his life will not threaten or dissolve his connection with his true first love (which for him and for all of us is the opposite-sex parent), he can begin to see the women in his life as they really are and for what they can realistically offer him. This clarity will help him find satisfaction for his adult self and he will become a more "present" mate.

Men Misunderstand Female Friendships Because They Aren't Women

From a guy's perspective, a girlfriend's focus on relationships, fashion, decor, and kids seems like just so much chitchat. From his position, the hours women spend on the telephone, the mall runs, and the coffee klatches are simply incomprehensible. And the way women depend on each other to listen to their problems and to help out can even seem exploitative.

The truth is that women see other women as sisters in their struggle through life's ups and downs. Their friendships evolve over availability and mutuality, and they provide the kind of support most men simply aren't ready to serve up.

Friendship, in psychoanalytic terms, is a relationship wherein the natural sexual and aggressive drives that everyone has are inhibited. We don't screw our friends, literally or figuratively.

Men don't get women's friendships because men's friendships are much more about rank. Perhaps because men may have stronger drives than women, their friendships are less collegial. The difficulty in abandoning "pecking order" may explain why sports and professional activities remain prominent points of discussion among most men.

Most Women Really Do Want a Man to Protect and Take Care of Them

If we were still living in caves, under siege from fanged beasts and rival Neanderthals, this principle would be far less controversial. In a world with security systems and supermarkets, the yen for a chest-beating he-man with a sizable club seems a bit outré.

Nevertheless, even though they don't want to be dragged by their hair back to the Stone Age, today's women usually don't seek out unemployed weaklings as husbands. Most still fall back on their anthropological legacy: they want guys whose attributes and assets can improve their lot in life and keep the wolves at bay. And if procreation is on the docket, they want ones whose genes will commingle into smart, attractive *Kinder*, and ones who can maintain the bank account during the diaper-duty years. It's not that women cannot support themselves, because they can. It's just that if a woman is in the market for a man, she'd like him to be supportive.

Too Much Love May Mean Hate;
Too Much Hate May Mean Love

People don't necessarily act as they feel, deep down inside, for defensive reasons. Onlookers are not always snowed by their behavior though. For example, they may comment, "Those two fight all the time. Why don't they just screw and get it over with?" Even though the sexual attraction is palpable, the pair continues to spat. Or as someone remarked of an acquaintance, "You know, the more she insists that she loves him and says that it is only his job that is the problem, the more I think she really just hates his guts."

Shrinks have a term for this behavior pattern. Acting the opposite of an actual feeling is called reaction-formation. Reaction-formationers don't just say the opposite of what they mean. They live it. They skirt conscious acknowledgment; in fact they are *unaware* of their internal emotions. They behave in opposition to them out of a fear that the emotions possess destructive power. People apply reaction-formation to whatever they fear— positive or negative, love or hate.

Try encouraging those in this dilemma to discuss their feelings. At first they may deny everything, couching their feelings in feeble justifications: "I can't hate him. Look at how well I treat him"; or by contrast, "I don't love him. Look at all the problems between us."

Following this thread of truth may eventually bring the whole garment of their feelings out to air. For example, a woman might acknowledge, "He represents the ultimate macho pig. If I admit how much I long for him, that makes a mockery of all my professed feminism." Or a commitment-phobe may feel deep down, "If I admit how much I love her, will I be obliged to marry her?" Or a married person, acknowledging real hostility, might ask, "If I feel that way, doesn't that mean I have to divorce him and destroy my family?" These conundrums, though still problematic, are at least honest.

Total Isolation Is Never Healthy and Adaptive

With the possible exception of ascetics living on ledges at high altitudes, no one *really* wants to be cut off from everything. "Leave me alone!" may be just another way of saying, "I only feel safe when I'm by myself." Abusive childhoods, ghastly traumas, and other myriad shocks quake and sever individuals from their fundamental tools for love and, indeed, the hope for love. Not only does the ability to love crumble, the pain can be so great that the very memory builds up a callused protective shell. Damaged people toughen and retreat ever further into aloneness. Their shield against intimacy grows by habit.

Solitary people come in many varieties. They may seem shy. They may seem curmudgeonly. They may even appear totally normal, but continually withdraw into their self-imposed isolation rather than relate to others. Even those who would like to overcome their solitude—whatever its variety—find it difficult to cease the behaviors that they have constructed to ward off intimacy. Their solitary habits become the "known" and forays out are the "unknown." The longer this continues the scarier and the less knowable the unknown seems.

I do not mean to suggest that everyone needs a husband or a wife or a lover. I do not mean people should not live alone. Some lone wolves get all the interaction they can handle through work and find they really require relative seclusion after hours, at least much of the time. A few phone calls and an outing here and there are enough to sate their emotional demands.

Relationships

In whatever amount, friends, family, and colleagues provide the close human contact that nurture and often challenge us to expand our emotional repertoire. The reciprocity that loving relationships provide allows us to stretch our hearts and fortify our connection with mankind and with ourselves. A loving circle of exchange that includes giving and taking is key to *fulfillment*.

MOVING FORWARD

History Repeats Itself,
Over and Over and Over . . .

The faces and the settings are different. But the reactions remain the same. Most individuals, if they're honest, find startling similarities in their thinking and feelings year after year. Trace the reactions of any one person to their incipience, and you'll find a core event and/or a core caregiver that precipitated the mindset and the way of dealing with it emotionally. Very often, the coping mechanism, though habituated, keeps the individual mired in pain. As long as troubling experience remains unconscious, it keeps churning out the same burn moods.

What is lovely, and inherently perfect, about continually bashing our heads against the same walls is this: Repetition is our psyche's effort to goad us into change.

Bringing the unconscious to consciousness is therapy's "pay dirt." Psychotherapists subtly (and not so subtly) get out the therapeutic backhoes and commence the unearthing process. Before long, they bare forgotten layers of emotional landscape. It's all very unsettling as memories resurface. Casting them in relationship to present events and seeing how they have shaped consistent feelings can be painful but transformative.

Other episodes—not just therapy—can dredge memories. Often memories surface under mundane circumstances or when one is touched by tenderness. Cataclysmic events provide the kind of upheaval that can really uncover stashed feelings. It's as though the eons—our own passing years—pile new experiences like sediment over our past. Undisturbed, the sediment gathers more layers and settles under the compression of demanding lives. Whether set off by an almost imperceptible event or a real emotional "earthquake," the surface can crack and shift the plated layers that have grown over early traumas. When this happens, watch out. When the unconscious rises to the conscious, it is *life altering.*

. . . But You *Can* Learn to Help Yourself—*Sometimes*

Everyone gnaws on his or her own paw from time to time. Shrinks call these itinerant worries neurotic anxieties. They may not stem from anything more major than the normal misunderstandings that characterize everyday life. For instance, you may worry that a coworker is displeased with something you did recently. Or someone's comment can make you aware that you could have been more sensitive, and you wonder, *Why wasn't I?* Even the public focus on psychology can cause you to throw some previously unruffled part of yourself under the magnifying glass where you'll be disturbed to find its glaring imperfection.

Though these incidental vexations could be worked out with a therapist, they do not necessarily require therapy. They may be the stuff of self-help books. Even though self-help books have limitations, readers can, *with resolve*, cultivate fresh thought patterns on their own.

Cleaning up mental habits is not the same as one-hour Martinizing. Commitment is not enough. It requires the kind of awareness and discipline that most of us simply can't supply for ourselves. Journals can be helpful. Sometimes strong support at home, from friends or from a group can provide the feedback necessary to keep new thought patterns on track. Whatever the structure, it is important that it provide regular mechanisms for measuring the strength and consistency of more healthful behavior.

Deep-seated anxieties that stem from traumas are another

ball of wax. They are harder to treat and usually require professional help. A good therapist can encourage patients to put words to events that may have been otherwise too horrendous to speak of. Unspoken traumas spread out like oil over water. Until they are recognized and mopped up, they continue to poison. The detox, which may be beyond self-help-book capabilities, can begin.

You Can Use Your Cortex
to Master Your Limbic System

This isn't choreography-talk direction for a South American party dance. The cortex is a powerful tool. It gathers new data, weighs it, sorts it, and generally behaves like any front end unit, putting input to use. With enough attention and direction, this part of our noggin can overcome the extravagant emotional urges that are buried deeper in our brains, in the limbic system. With the cortex back in charge, we need not act primitive anymore.

All the cortex has to do is make good decisions. All the limbic system has to do is stand by, waiting to see what the good decisions bring about. It sounds easy. Yet, most of us operate this way but intermittently, and usually only under the supervision of a costly therapist. Instead we allow emotions to blur good judgment. Acting on our feelings without thinking is the same as giving the limbic too much rein. And we all know that too much rein leads to tripping.

Experiment with this on your own. Start with paying attention to what triggers your emotional responses: He does so and so; you get weepy, then have a fit. She does so and so; you get accusatory, then blow up. If these are not your scenarios, insert scenarios that sound familiar. Most people know their own pattern, and using the great central processing unit called their brain, they can begin to recognize their own buttons. It's as simple as this: When you notice that you're yelling, blubbering, or fulminating, stop for a sec, and note why. Search your memory for antecedents. Then, next time that same "why" occurs, restrain the extravagant response with a broadened perspective. Imagine that a jury of twelve of your peers is assessing the situation for you. Likely, they'd suggest a more expansive and less destructive response.

New experience changes the limbic reaction. And the cortex can initiate that experience when it receives new knowledge. So, relying *only on logic,* decide what response would be different from, and preferable to, the one that usually spontaneously erupts. Then try it, even if you doubt its effectiveness. If your explosive response were effective, you wouldn't have to detonate it so frequently. Also, it would only be effective if it actually made you feel more emotionally stable . . . and it doesn't.

You'll have to be very attentive to keep the limbic in check. But try it once. Try it twice. Soon your limbic will traffic events with a fresh repertory of emotions. Awareness gives you opportunities, but it's up to you to take them.

Neutrality, Though Often Desired, Is Difficult to Achieve

Intelligence with impartiality is a potent mix, more common in gods than in the everyman. That is because gods don't need anything. Real life seems to produce an automatic desire to establish a position in relationship to what is going on. Past events can't help but bias what follows, and since we of the flesh and blood are all saps for transference, complete neutrality is almost impossible to achieve. Even people who have been through all kinds of analysis and have been trained to recognize where they distort reality find it hard to shake preconceptions. Yet if one can maintain more detachment, more aspects of a situation will be apparent. And more potentially helpful avenues will open.

Here, it is imperative to remember that the therapeutic role does not call for control or judgment. Shrinks work reciprocally, listening and questioning, rather than concluding. The shrink and the patient are trying to get at the truth together. The listener's neutrality forces the patient, or the person expressing himself or herself, to generate decision making and conflict resolution from within. At a fork in the road, giving advice just isn't as helpful as making a qualified suggestion or sharing a knowledge base. If, by contrast, one judges, taking sides in an internal conflict, it undermines the conflicted person's self-reliance. They may stubbornly take the other side. Or they may be cowed into following along, increasing their dependency.

Ideally, achieving emotional health is a self-discovery process, a way of learning to solve problems internally. This process isn't the slam dunk of more fascistic assistance—such as a god might dole out—but it achieves a far more enduring transformation for the patient.

A Goal-Directed Focus
Can Lead to Poor Results

It's usually okay to keep one eye on the prize, but you'd better keep the other on the process that will lead there. Sometimes the process may require you to ignore the goal entirely. As winners will very often tell you, the *process* is the most important aspect of achievement. Focusing on end results often gets poor results. But, in contrast, directing positive energy into where you are along the way can get good results. Be "where you are" as well as you can be.

Examples: The person who is trying to diet gains weight. That obsession with calories and shedding tonnage may override the more important focus on improved lifestyle. Getting off one's duff and seeking out exercise, nourishing relationships, pleasureful pastimes, a better job, etc., will lead to happiness. Then weight loss will occur naturally.

The person who is trying to sleep never drops off. Insomniacs stay awake to ask over and again, "When am I going to go to sleep?" More rested are those who relax, imagine a tranquil scene, and enjoy the moment of waiting to drop off.

The person who obsesses about making money stays impoverished. In lieu of counting how many pennies come and go each day, why not invest energy in activities that are both productive and enjoyable. Take the long view.

Here is another example: The man who focuses on maintaining his erection loses it. The man who forgets his erection and focuses on the pleasures of sexual intimacy, paradoxically, stays erect.

How about the person who is trying to achieve orgasm and doesn't? In shrink-speak, their *parasympathetics get overridden by their sympathetics*. That means that they are thinking too much about something that demands feeling. The treatment is to stop "trying" and indulge in the sensations. Touch, movement, and sharing are the process. They lead to the goal.

These poor devils are not freaks; they are the everyman. We all fall prey to shortcutting the process simply because it is human.

Therefore, the best counsel is to move the focus, to take a tack that distracts from the issue at hand and devotes mental faculties to other ends. This repositioning may seem counterintuitive, moving the attention off the goal as it does. But it usually works. It's not the destination; it's the voyage!

It Is the Experience That Heals,
Not Just the Insight . . .

Insights are a dime a dozen. Real change, on the other hand, is harder to come by and impressive when it occurs. Pop psychology, step programs, the media, etc., treat us to a long buffet of fresh intelligence about our stress, our angst, our phobias, and so on. We're completely saturated with reasons for being screwed up. What this psycho-bath doesn't automatically do is cure us. That requires *work*. And work does not occur in a vacuum. We have to get out there and interact, testing what we've learned with others. You can't sit in a corner until you become a good tennis player and then go to Wimbledon. You have to learn by doing.

We balk. Well-inured psychological defenses, developed over a lifetime, keep us from recognizing what needs to be done. We try to blame others. We are afraid. Whatever. All this stalling seldom improves matters, and that's why people so often need shrinks. Without shrinks to hold their feet to the fire, people might not do, or might not know how to do, the painful work. Good psychotherapists help patients identify stumbling blocks that they themselves have not, even with a lot of reading. Likewise, therapeutic relationships show how to overcome obstacles that aren't so easy to negotiate with self-treatment.

It doesn't have to be a therapist doing the coaching. Research reveals that healthy nonprofessionals can sometimes inadvertently provide psychotherapy as well as those with advanced degrees. From a loving "other" perspective, they can draw the other person toward higher awareness.

Again though, whether patient or friend, each of us has to work beyond the phase during which we had the insight personally. Something akin to a thunderbolt can slap us, but the realization is incidental until put into practice. Visits to the shrink can train for real-life interaction. But it is out there in the trenches with friends, family, and coworkers that we test and perfect personal growth. Real life brings on maturity in ways that psychotherapy alone cannot provide.

. . . Therefore, Intimate Relationships Are Great Therapy

Cuddling up in the pillows with a relationship book is not the same as dating. And it's a far cry from marriage. It has limitations, some of which we pointed out in the previous principle. All the reading in the world pales in comparison to the growth that emanates from a partner who acts and talks back. That's what keeps people hankering after companionship, no matter how challenging. The one-on-one is not always pretty, and it can be a whole lot more painful than turning pages. But it gets results!

Involvement with an intimate partner unpacks all the stored psychology of our upbringing. Usually without recognizing that we are doing so, we are inevitably attracted to people who allow us to revisit our childhood issues, as I've said elsewhere. When we fall in love, we begin testing those building blocks of our youth to observe whether we have learned to overcome their weaknesses and put them together in solid ways.

Sex ups the ante. It exposes people's vulnerability in ways that buttoned-up life doesn't. Intimacy is, well, intimate. Its give-and-take can whip up a real tempest of unwieldy feelings—anxiety, expectations, disappointment, frustration, anger, fear, and many more—driving participants into states of which they may not have known they were capable. The healthier the lovers, the better they can weather the feelings that accompany emotionally charged exchanges of body fluid.

The more committed the relationship, the more intense its therapeutic value. People can go through a series of uncommitted relationships, revisiting more or less the same level of emotion every time. It is when they push or are pushed into binding arrangements that the exploration of their psyche deepens.

Romances and marriages often foster meaningful change. They provide a real-life testing ground for principles readers have explored in books. But in therapeutic terms, whether the structures we create in intimate relationships work or don't work is less important than whether we attempt the relationships in the first place. The attempts demonstrate a willingness to get off the sofa and brave the monumental task of growing beyond our own frailties. Sometimes, frequently in fact, relationships' less healthy aspects push participants to explore buried issues or new psychological frontiers. More positively, they add that interactive human element that can't be found on a shelf.

Any other relationship—be it with friends, family, therapist—presents dynamic opportunities to evaluate one's role in real-life terms. But the intimate relationship, characteristically, packs the most punch.

MARRIAGE

Marriage Is to "Living Together" As Apples Are to Oranges

Whether we're talking cohabitation or fruits, *distinctions are differences*. Marriage today seems ever less permanent with the growing divorce rate. Yet there remain centuries of cultural pressure behind the marriage contract. Marriage means you are "locked in." And if you don't believe it, talk to anyone who has been to divorce court, especially if they have children. Getting out of a marriage is a far cry from loading up the U-Haul.

People who live together with a sense of permanency without saying "I do" sometimes rationalize that they don't need a piece of paper to prove they are married. Well, time to blow the cobwebs out of the cerebrum! Accept it or not, in cohabitation in which there is no piece of paper, one of the partners, if not both, may have cold feet.

This does not undermine the worth of shacking up. It can be wonderful. Cohabitation only deteriorates when the partners have different expectations about the relationship. One person, or both, may see living together as a precursor to marriage, expecting that resolving snags about toilet paper and finances will lead inevitably to the altar. But if one partner sees marriage on the horizon and the other sees a fenceless frontier, problems are nigh. That's what sends people scurrying for couples counseling. Or gulping vodka and chocolate.

Marriage Is Not a Happy Ending;
It Is Only the Beginning . . .

If living together forever were a cake walk, we wouldn't have to make vows. We wouldn't have to "work" at it. The likelihood of any two people snuggling into a household seamlessly is remote. Marriage always requires adjustment and compromise. Happily, the upsides are often sufficient to overshadow the downsides. And a certain amount of shuffling and reshuffling can result in a marriage that is not only livable but rewarding. That this happens so infrequently is no surprise though.

Unlike blood relatives, we *choose* our spouses. So we can't pawn off responsibility for our connubial discontent on our parents or siblings. Our predicament is entirely our own fault. Marriage forces the trials we've carried around since childhood into an adult theater. This is an exciting if irritating event, because as adults, we no longer need to accept victimhood. Of course, many fail to take the opportunity and may slog through married life as an extension of their childhood selves.

Marriages can "re-create" us. That other human we married brings another upbringing and another set of genes to the household. A fresh view. As many challenges as occur individually are doubled in a marriage. When they come up—which is all the time—husbands and wives can go through each other's closets, figuratively, determining which aspects to use, which to abandon, and which to overhaul. Often—over fifty percent of the time—couples get fed up with this emotionally demanding re-creation and dial the divorce attorney.

. . . And It Is Easier to Say What Marriage Is Not Than What It Is

As a social and cultural convention, marriage is a shapeless tangle—complicated, changing, and as easy to generalize about as weather. The psychological community may be as much in the dark about marriage as everyone else. Historically, shrinks have done a poor job of telling patients what it can be, possibly because personal experience and clinical practice have proven only that its description is elusive.

Usually, love and high hopes can get couples to take that trip down the aisle. People also gravitate to marriage for entirely practical reasons that have to do with money, solidarity, security, and children. Familiarity is another reason. As children we felt "locked in" and marriage is the adult formula for getting "locked in" anew. Commitments build stability. In addition, most of us grew up in married households and merely by habit we are inclined to re-create this structure, particularly if there is approbation from our families, not to mention nudging, in support of the move.

Sex may get people into marriages, but it is rarely the sustaining ingredient. Nor is easy conflict resolution a reason for marrying, as many couples develop a routine that relies little on complete resolution. Rather, it is family habit, momentum, and affection that bind couples together. After a certain interval, their chemistry gives them a sort of molecular integrity that, however volatile, endures unless powerful catalysts arrive to sever it. For most, it is easier (not to mention cheaper) to stay married than to cast off into an indefinite future. For at least half of the population, getting unmarried is just too much trouble.

There Can Only Be One "Number One" in a Marriage

Don't get married unless you are willing to place your spouse at the center of your happiness. Otherwise, the fur will fly.

Once there are children, this prioritizing becomes even more important, for the children's sake as well as that of mothers and fathers. Although the child who succeeds in pulling one parent away from the other may feel empowered, ultimately it will create lasting obstacles to commitment in their own future. Moreover, children need contented parents who can provide emotional support to them and to each other without jealousy or hostility. Without this fundamental security, kids develop no internal place of refuge. When they consult their "inner family" they find flux and acrimony. They may go through life trying to build confidence by luring people away from existing relationships into their camp.

When families find a parent and children pitted against the other parent, it is a time of crisis, not a way of life.

The caveat to keep one's mate at the fulcrum becomes especially challenging in stepfamilies. Feelings of guilt about divorce and what it has inflicted on the children may naturally incline parents to side with their biological children instead of their spouses. Or stepparents may interpret the relationship between their spouses and their biological children as a menace to their own sovereignty. Either way, problems escalate because the central bond between husband and wife is shaky.

For this reason, it is critical for a divorced parent who is thinking of remarrying to investigate his or her lover's solidarity with the existing parenting commitment. The more children there are, the trickier this is, as it is likely the children will differ in their feelings toward the replacement for their birth parent. The *Brady Bunch* aside, know that this is hardly ever easy.

You Can't Change Your Spouse

No doubt about it, the Pygmalion impulse is compelling. Who wouldn't want the opportunity to fashion the ideal mate? We've all imagined him . . . or her. We meet someone with potential, but they have a few flaws. Sensing the diamond in the rough, we get out the chisel. We set about redressing, retraining, retrieving, and generally overhauling that person, hoping through constant vigilance, in varying degrees of subtlety, to create our personal paragon.

The problem with these flights of creativity, as they involve already fully formed creatures, is that they work against accomplishing the very love we hope to achieve. Not ironically, intimacy in reformation-style relationships tends to underwhelm. No one wants to become a project for Mr. or Mrs. Fix-It. Lovemaking should be about lovemaking, not an exercise in faultfinding or even an occasion to tighten loose screws.

Many marital therapists counsel an "acceptance and adaptation" approach. This calls for putting down the magnifying glass you've held over your partner and picking up the mirror. Face yourself honestly. You wanted a design project? Pursue your own goals. Create your own you. You may inspire your partner to greater efforts through your attention to your own flaws.

By setting aside the Partner Improvement Agenda, you'll observe your spouse for the person he or she really is. Look. Listen. This is the person you married. You may wake up one day and marvel at the changes that have taken place in your husband or wife. Or you may not. But chances are that any transformation will happen organically, and much more pleasantly, if you let it emerge without force. Save your flair for remodeling for the house.

Couples Tend to Socialize with Couples and Singles with Singles

If your marital status precludes you from social engagements, take it as a compliment. It may be that your peers are envious of you, and not entirely comfy or secure in their present circumstances.

Married couples sometimes jostle single people's sense of happiness because they represent what being single lacks—family, security, love, and togetherness. Conversely, singles of either sex may threaten matrimonial bliss because they are still freewheeling. Their liberty, not to mention their availability, can appear tantalizing to all people who are naturally ambivalent in their marriages. The instability both these syndromes introduce may be just too unnerving to invite into a social setting. Hence, wanting to have a relaxed time keeps people socializing with others of their ilk.

Pulling an extra person into a preexisting relationship—such as a spouse into a close friendship or a close friend into a marriage—isn't easy. Just because two people are crazy about each other, either as friends or spouses, doesn't mean the third person will automatically fit in. Jealousy, insecurity, or even indifference is possible. It is so ticklish that many just avoid it.

Another more practical aspect governs who socializes with whom: time. People with families simply do not have the same number of hours in their days as people who do not because so many of those hours are allocated to others, especially when children are involved. Furthermore, social occasions tend to materialize spontaneously and more conveniently among people who keep similar schedules and do similar activities.

Parenthood Is Not for Everyone

Some folks just aren't cut from the Ma and Pa cloth. Professional challenges and rewards, an adventurous spirit, and anticipated financial strain can keep men and women clinging to their contraceptives. They may decide—with some justification—that there are already too many people. Others are reluctant to relinquish self-absorption in favor of the vicariousness which they imagine parenthood demands. People who require space and people who require order know they'd be miserable as parents. Older siblings from large families—particularly in latchkey circumstances—may have had more than their fill of parenting by the time they reach adulthood.

When only one half of a partnership is opposed to parenthood, problems can escalate in syncopation with the tick of the woman's "biological clock." This conflict may require more compromise than almost any other in a relationship and can be a challenge that even intense love cannot overcome.

The decision to not have children rests most heavily on women, as their childbearing years are, unlike men's, limited. Men can always make the decision mañana. So the debate about whether to have children or not is anything but fair. Women who pursue other goals through their childbearing years often need to be reminded in midlife of the fruit of their labor and its impact on the larger community. Pride can lessen any misgivings about having forgone parenthood.

Finally, we all know couples who seem blissfully content in

their childless but intimate and compatible marriages. Though they may get an earful of cultural pressure about their decision, parenthood is a personal decision. Self-knowledge has led them to avoid a path that would frustrate their independence and possibly challenge their relationship.

An Extramarital Affair Is Itself Less Important Than What Led to It . . .

Shrinks are often more like the stereotypical European when it comes to infidelity. They may accept it as an occasional inevitability. This is not meant to undermine the sanctity of marital promises, but merely to point out that transgressions are human. Remember? This book teaches how to think like a shrink, not react like a spouse. Like it or not, the vast majority have an extramarital liaison at one time or another during their marriage.

Adulterers come in two varieties: those who don't want to be caught and those who do. Clever people who want to keep their families intact limit their infidelity to brief flings, often out of town. That way their libidinous vagaries won't impact their marriages, or so they reason. These sorts of affairs may have nothing to do with the spousal relationship but are instead momentary lapses in self-control. Men are especially, though not exclusively, susceptible to what may be purely sexual slip-ups. Then again, repeated sexual sprees can be an avoidance of issues at home. As we learn from our politicians, it's all about not getting caught.

In the other camp are the lemmings. People who parade their infidelity in full view of the pack are bent on destruction, not just of their own lives but of their families' lives. They may have a masochistic relationship with their spouses. Or if not, by flaunting their affairs, they are inviting change and paving an unavoidable road away from their marriages.

In either case, real determinants led to what seems like the betrayal. It didn't just happen. Humans will attempt to meet their needs, especially when having unanswered needs seems unnecessary or becomes intolerable. The parties involved—the faithless spouse, the cuckolded spouse, and the intervening lover—all have lives that are at least partially unlivable.

. . . And Also Less Important Than What Comes After It

When someone gets caught with their pants down, it is not just an apocalypse. It's often an opportunity! It forces the situation to a head. Many people feel an extramarital affair is an inexcusable treachery, a violation for which the only response is the utter end, and as retributive and bloody an end as possible. Though certainly where matters of the heart are concerned this is an understandable reaction, it overlooks the revelations that the event has exposed.

Though the inconstant partner may be in the less defensible position, he or she is not always entirely culpable. The "cheated" husband or wife very often plays a part, consciously or unconsciously, in bringing about the infidelity. Even when the cheater is an irrevocable ass, the victim must certainly ask profound questions about what attracted him or her to such a person to begin with. And those questions are just the initial ones in a deeper investigation into the past, both with the spouse and before.

Though blaming and vindictiveness feel good in the short term, neither have staying power when it comes to personal growth. Both wife and husband will profit from examining what transpired, either together or apart. If, instead, they opt not to throw their own role under the microscope, the unhappy pattern will repeat. A few months or years later, they'll find themselves confronted with more inconstancy, and a fresh opportunity to find out why.

Whether their life theme is abandonment or abuse or narcissism or whatever, they will continue to live it, either with the spouse or with others, unless they make a concerted effort to switch themes. This is usually no snap, and requires tireless work, often accompanied by therapy. Couples who profit from the hellfire can use it to forge a new course for the future. Just ask Hillary.

Kids Keep Marriages Together

The physical and financial demands of raising a family are Herculean—more than most parents can provide singly. To that extent, especially in a child's first years, marriage makes sense. One parent spends most of her time bent over by either averting or cleaning up after disasters. (This isn't always the woman, just usually.) The other slogs away at the office, trying to afford a bigger backyard and padding the college fund. Both parents are driven as if possessed by an infatuation that overtook them the minute they slapped eyes on their offspring. Both dream only intermittently of romance. They don't have time. And they are busy loving the person who looks at them only with love and never with incrimination—their child.

I'm not making a moral injunction here that couples should stay together for the kids. Instead, I am saying that successful marriages rest on common goals, common interests, and common values. The innocent young creatures who are in a sense the *result* of marriage can, and often do, become a *common cause* of marriage. Kids provide the motivation to keep marriage from unraveling. Parenting reinforces growth in the family setting because it is so much about acceptance, compromise, and adaptation.

The momentum of keeping it all together can keep it together, for a decade or two, until the children are more independent or until they depart. At that point, many unions crumble, one or the other or both spouses flapping out of the empty nest like bats out of hell. Not always though. Sometimes, if they can weather the adjustment, couples find that without kids they still really enjoy each other, and caring about their adult children's welfare is still a common goal.

Divorce Doesn't Solve Everything and Usually Introduces New Challenges

A divorce is an ending, but it is not *the* end. It is an intermediate step. Marriage exposes you to your strengths, weaknesses, and blind spots like no other medium. And those will not magically evaporate once you rid your life of the irksome other. They are your own. And you just can't shake them. Plus, since divorce involves money and the law, it intensifies both spouses' emotions in ways inconceivable until you're on your way to court.

You can learn much, more than you could ever learn in one hundred years of analysis, if you sort through the exposures marriage has afforded before you hightail it out into a pasture that may not necessarily be greener. Look for life lessons. If you understand and fully accept how much of your unhappiness is your own responsibility, you may see ways to transmute it within the relationship you are already in. It's practically a law that people who go blithely forth into subsequent relationships without looking carefully at the reasons that unfurled their marriages will suffer in the same ways over again.

Remember, no life is a bowl of cherries. No life is without conflict and hurt. Conflict and hurt push us to discard outgrown attitudes and behaviors, then forge new, healthier ways of being with ourselves and with others. The step that comes as one considers divorce can be immensely rewarding, but only if one acts with self-responsibility, not with blame.

Further, when kids are involved, it's important to acknowledge that divorce rarely rids one's life of the once-loved other parent. The ex is often nearby with the same irksome traits that made the marriage unlivable. Contact, which happens every time you pass the children back and forth, can bring back all the gnashing and bashing anew. Divorced parents get ample opportunities, as the years and contact go forward, to try fresh and more healthful approaches to dealing with this fountain of irritation and bitterness.

COMMUNICATION

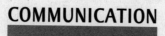

Actions Speak Louder Than Words

Yack. Yack. Yack. Getting feelings off your chest may seem as if it will lighten your load, but if the load still lingers, there may be problems that communication alone just can't mend. Communication is limited. People need to rework their *attitudes* as well. Without attitude changes, bared feelings add controversy to an interaction instead of allaying it. The other person can intensify the weightiness of your topic further and send it back toward you, catapulting its heavy contents into dangerous volley.

We have been taught that open expression will lead to resolution and greater intimacy. But this is not always the case, especially when the expression demands that the other person change. Nothing is more toxic than imposed qualifiers such as "If you love me, you will amend your ways since *such and such* annoys me." This view overlooks the interpersonal dynamic. No one arrives in a relationship without a past or without his or her own agenda. Though it seems ironic, sometimes willingness to accept another person's shortcomings is a more powerful move toward resolution than talking about them will ever be.

In a psychological climate that favors increased gab, we too often forget the old homily "Actions speak louder than words." The heavier the topic, the more important this may be. My advice is not only to think before you speak; it is to *do* before you speak. The action may be something you do for the other person that will shift feelings positively. Or it may be something you do on your own. Consider what changes you can make in your *own* life that will take the heat off the topic. Intense feelings have origins that predate the relationship you are in, so likely there is personal work to do that will ease the pressure of those feelings. The work may be therapy. It may be developing nurturing regimes and interests that do not demand so much of others. Either way, as an alternative to endless arguments, try this: Act first, communicate later.

If You Really Want to Relate,
Let People Free Associate

"Just say whatever thoughts come into your mind without censoring them." For the listener, this directive can be a ticket to an excursion through a private wonderland complete with a rabbit-hole-speed descent, Mad Hatter's tea-party-style conversation, and Queen of Hearts rampage.

The main advantage of "free association" is that it is *free*. And by that, I mean free of the impediments and pitfalls that come when the speaker is worried about being interrupted or judged. If the speaker is anxious about having to hold the listener's attention, he or she may "perform" self-consciously. Or if worrying about being criticized is a factor, the soliloquy will be guarded, with all defense systems activated. The revelations won't confer anything too personal. And you, the listener, will have to "read" the truth through a scrim of self-protective mechanisms, developed over a lifetime of posturing.

However, the time to initiate healing doesn't have to wait for more information. As we all know from personal experience, the issues are often traumatic, and always redundant. That's how they became issues. Something painful happened once. Then it happened again. Right after it happened a third time, it began to happen a fourth. That's what sends people scurrying to shrinks.

I have personally come to the conclusion that the free association technique can be abbreviated with positive results. The heart of brief-treatment success stories is the ability to focus people on their key conflicts. When a familiar issue emerges out of free association, help them recognize it. In time, the free associater will learn to spot their own issues as they come up. This is far less tedious for the listener and more expeditious for the patient.

Asking Is More Effective Than Telling

Shrinks are masters of the interrogative. They perpetuate the patient's exposition and direct his or her growth with a steady stream of questions. When you hear a television or movie shrink repeatedly ask, "How did that make you feel?" it may be funny and seem really obvious. But the humor doesn't diminish the fact that the technique is also very valuable and even essential.

This is because lack of awareness isn't always just "lack." When it comes to big issues, the oversights can stem from the *inability* or even *refusal* to be aware. So sharing an insight isn't as easy as just revealing it. You have to burrow through what can be a nearly impenetrable wall of biased thinking. Shrinks have found that a query works better than a statement.

Take, for example, the statement of a fifty-year-old mother of two who declares to a thirty-five-year-old man, "You are aggressive with women in authority because your mother was a controlling, castrating woman who left you totally insecure." That's going to go over like a lead balloon.

She could gently inquire instead, "Do you think that when you are with women in authority you feel out of control and that you can then be aggressive verbally to take back that control? Could those feelings have anything to do with your mother, whom you have described as controlling?"

It makes sense, of course, because by allowing someone to answer a question, you allow them to stay in charge of themselves, even when you are subtly or not so subtly guiding the course of inquiry. From their standpoint, this means facing the mirror rather than defending against an adversary. This is especially necessary, and especially potent, with people who harbor memories of abuse.

Moreover, the asking introduces a topic that can be passed back and forth, examined in more depth. The passing will repeat and underscore its truth with a power that a brute declaration will never achieve.

Beware Unsolicited Denials

"I don't hate my mother," he stammers.
"I don't care about money," she blurts.

Subjects that come up unsolicited, framed as denials such as "I'm not jealous," or "I *never* lie," carry a hodgepodge of issues in tow. When you receive disclosures such as these without invitation, the topic is usually a hot one and the discloser is sheepish.

Just try getting the person who doesn't hate Mom to expand on her many attributes and in due course you'll get an earful of criticism against her. Or ask the person for whom money is no object to describe the financial situation in question. There may be dollar-themed concerns complete with spreadsheets, budgets, and actuary tables for every penny spent. Don't reject what unsolicited deniers say out loud. It will be difficult to break through the stronghold of their outward convictions with an aggressive assault. Saying "Bullshit," for example, may get you nowhere. A good policy is to bide your time, and watch how they act. Don't press. If, after six or eight hours, they don't hang themselves with their own rope, you might try asking, "Why did you say that?" Over time, they may, however inadvertently, reveal the momentary deceitful mother-loathing miser aspect (in these examples) of their unconscious that caused them to make such grandiose denials to begin with.

Defense Mechanisms May Be Inauthentic

Jeff Goldblum delivers my favorite line from the movie *The Big Chill:* "Where would any of us be without a good rationalization?" We buffer every decision we make with a reason. It's almost as if we anticipate that someone is going to ask why we do what we do. And to some extent our own worth depends on the ability to supply plausible logic to our actions.

One of the most popular forms of defense, particularly for unhealthy or felonious behaviors, is *denial*. Although a policy of "it isn't happening" is easy in the short term, it takes a lot of energy to sustain long-term. Perpetuating denial over a sequence of changing circumstances can exhaust even the most ingenuous denier.

Devaluing, a favorite defense for egotists, diminishes the road not taken. It works well for those who don't mind cutting off their noses to spite their faces.

Idealizing is a sort of optimist's version of denial. Idealizers can be led down any garden path. They fall easy prey to fast talkers. Every decision springs from a confidence in the superlative nature of the guru or whatever else they blindly admire.

Splitting is a combination of devaluing and idealizing. It divides issues into absolute good and absolute bad. Splitters arbitrarily sort people into villains and heroes, events into black and white. So doing leaves the parts of life that are neither here nor there, but in the gray zone, unexamined.

All these defense mechanisms rob individuals of power and stability for one obvious reason: *They're not true.*

What People Say Is Sometimes Less Important Than Why They Are Saying It . . .

Just as psychics observe with their "third eye," psychiatrists listen with their "third ear." So can you. It's a way of eavesdropping on the speaker's intent, while at once being audience to their subject, and here's how it works.

People never fail to bring up topics that reflect how they are feeling at that moment, and they deliver them in a way to impact the situation. Consciously, they may not realize that they are being so expressive. Their words may seem no more than chitchat or revelatory description. Nonetheless, there is always a less conscious desire behind every delivery and expression. Remember, people communicate because they want results!

To determine what those results may be, an emotionally stable listener has only to assess how what is being said makes them feel. Does the discussion make you feel needed? Thwarted? Trusted? Railroaded? Enlightened? Bored? The feeling is a direct response to the speaker's often-unconscious intention. As open-mindedly as possible, ask yourself, "Why is this person telling me this?" or "Why are they trying to make me feel this way?" And afterward, "What does this feeling tell me about how *they* are feeling?"

To test your third ear, you will need to confirm whatever you come up with as being accurate. The best way to corroborate your impression is to pose the question therapists so often ask, "How did this make you feel?" to the other person. This approach is less aggressive than stating your impression, and gives the person addressing you the opportunity to reveal another layer of intentions without being cut off at the pass by your *own* often-unconscious intention.

Let's say, on the other hand, you can't restrain yourself from baring your feelings. If your feelings are exaggerated, say a strong response of either elation or revulsion, it may mean that you are not the paragon of emotional stability that you thought you were. Perhaps, rather than experimenting with your third ear, you should reevaluate your own issues, especially if you can't say why your response is so out of proportion.

. . . For Instance, We Can Tell a Lot About People by the Way They Say Goodbye

The most telling minute of many interactions is the final minute. There are innumerable ways of sallying forth, from a breezy "Goodbye" to "Oh, I forgot to tell you I have cancer" to those toodle-oos that take a toll like the flu. Each reveals a lot about the people parting, intelligence that may not have been evident in the rest of the exchange.

Every departure has vestiges of separation anxiety, worse by degrees for some than for others. Is it a little or a lot? Paying attention to people as they turn heel quantifies that anxiety.

Imagine two babies, both about two years old, both experimenting with moving independently of their mothers. One mother is loving and supportive. The other is anxious and worried. The first baby learns that going away is okay. The second learns that departures are nervous-making. Those babies grow up into adults whose goodbyes reflect that early childhood experience.

We all know people who cling like a Post-it or wait until the last second to announce pivotal issues. Most of us have done it. A brandishing of neediness suggests a core hope that the listener will not go away and may be tied to unrelated memories of desertion. On the other hand, others don't bring up controversial topics until their foot is out the door because they just don't feel up to it. With no time for discussion, and much less time for resolution, maybe no one will notice they are apprehensive. A knack for speedy exits allows them to hightail it without having to explore topics they're not ready to explore, or leave before they are rejected.

More so than hellos, more so than the body of the get-together, goodbyes demonstrate levels of self-confidence, understanding, rapport, connection, and trust.

OUTWARD APPEARANCES

The Best Defense Is a Good Offense

No one is better at bombardment than someone with an Achilles' heel to defend. The threat doesn't even need to be real. Very often it is just anticipated. So determined are the inadequate to avoid seeing their weakness exposed that they mount and launch insults faster than a howitzer. Maybe their onlookers will be so busy defending themselves from the hail of abuse that they won't notice the Napoleonic complex at the source.

Importantly, the complex is very often unconscious. The attacker who identifies weakness in others frequently does not recognize his or her own weakness. The defense is therefore against self-knowledge. The offense can prevent the defensive person as well as others from learning the truth.

Though often on the mark with criticism and imposing to others, the offender's behavior seldom mitigates his or her own anxiety, since that would only arrive with potency. So the siege never stops.

By "potency," I don't necessarily mean sexual potency. I mean self-confidence as reflected in any field of endeavor. An attack can only cloak the impotency. But insightful offensiveness is a hard habit to kick. Impotency, in the hands of smart, sick egomaniacs, is what big wars are made of.

Sometimes if these defensive types can be led to recognize that they are angry, or that their criticism resembles a characteristic that they themselves have, they can learn to curb their assaults and concentrate instead on their own struggles.

Once-Traumatized People May Develop a Stubborn Need to Control

Whereas a person's body can be invaded and afflicted, even repeatedly, the mind may remain its own domain. This idea is a noted refuge for survivors of the Holocaust and other life-overturning tortures. To paraphrase Holocaust survivor Victor Frankel: You can do what you want to my body, but you can't take away my will.

Often, the insistence that one retain absolute power over oneself grows disproportionate to reason, so much so that even well-intended guidance isn't heeded. That is to say, traumatized people may not be able to take any advice, even advice that is in their best interest, like taking out the trash or paying their taxes in a timely manner. For them, doing what someone else says is tantamount to giving up entirely, and returning to the feelings of helplessness that overtook them during the trauma. Hence, they will unreasonably resist, no matter how counterproductive.

It is not uncommon to find traumatized people gambling away their assets or trading stocks too often or eating too much ice cream. Only if and when they come to realize that their sometimes self-destructive behavior is a residual of trauma can they begin to change. Naturally, they may not be willing to accept this revelation unsolicited, as accepting it would be identical to forfeiting their solidarity with themselves.

Emotions Are Harmless;
It Is Behavior That Can Harm

Wanting someone to drop dead is not the same as killing them. And though many people believe that the dastardly thought alone is a ticket to hell, it isn't really. It is just an inner voice of frustration . . . one that deserves not to be acted upon but recognized.

One can always stash the murderous mulling within, unexamined. Most people do. But then they go through life vaguely embittered because they're sitting on a bubbling cauldron of unexpressed loathing. And repressing such sentiments isn't good for your mental health or your physical health. This cauldron is a hot source of dis-ease.

A better option is to take note: Strong antipathy presents the occasion to mine the origins of the ill feelings. Likely, a person or incident brings out your hostility because it reminds you of a previous occasion in which you took it in the teeth. As you begin to understand the antecedents that make you so prone to ill will, you can better organize your way of thinking about the object or objects of your scorn. Take, for instance, an unreliable friend, a selfish husband, a critical boss, or a usurious lover. Contact with any one of them might result in adversarial feelings. *Why* do they irritate *you* so much? That is the fundamental question.

Everyone has buttons and they sometimes get pushed. But that doesn't mean you have to commence target practice or contaminate your foe's water supply. It would be far more productive to scratch below present circumstances and figure out what put you and this person in the same arena to begin with. The situation angers you because it reminds you of earlier situations in which you were also powerless. Unconscious desire to overcome your ongoing victimhood has, in a sense, put you in front of this occasion as an opportunity for resolution.

Consider a ball rolling down the stairs. Looking at the ball, there is an inevitability to its descent, just as there is a perceived inevitability to the victimhood you or someone you know may be experiencing. But there is another way of looking at the ball and stairs, and at the victimhood. Think of the stairs coming up, one after another, to meet the ball.

You can shift the perception of your situation to be less fatalistic too. There are steps you can now take, that you could not take then, to protect yourself from the negative repercussions of contact with this person. It is important not to feel defeatist here, and to move beyond any fatalism you may have routinized since childhood, but with appropriately expressed anger. Anger may strengthen your position if you are right!

Sometimes, the simplest actions, such as saying, "That is not acceptable," or "Don't treat me this way," or "I'm sorry, but this doesn't work for me," can completely alter a self-perpetuated pattern of subjugation, particularly if they can be made without the demand or expectation that the other person will automatically throw a parade in your honor.

The adversary's response is far less important than your new commitment to express your displeasure out loud. Even if you do not get your own way, these steps may increase your feeling of power over the situation and make you less likely to feel inflamed. With this insight, you'll find that you are better positioned to deflect. You will have fewer buttons. And better things to do.

Be direct.

Charmers Can Be Manipulative

People who don't bully but still get their way may have other methods, like charm. They fawn. They sizzle. They dazzle. Naturally eloquent, they may even be genuine. But if the overall desire is to dominate any given exchange, be it with one or two intimates or a whole stadium's worth of strangers, the charm they exude may be calculated.

Excessive charmers may need more than approval. They may need adoration. They may need to feel superior. They may need to know that at any given moment the situation and the people in it are entirely in their hands, dancing like puppets on strings tied to their whims. Why? Because during some previous period, usually childhood, they felt out of control and unacknowledged. Charm becomes, for them, a tool for squeezing what they want from others. Charmers make good rock stars.

Involvement with others, or the appearance thereof, may mask their deeper feelings of neediness or envy. However, involvement does not mend them. The more attention they wrest, the higher they rev. They can't help themselves. In the end, they are rarely satisfied and often disconsolate. Their real requirement is for the kind of love that does not hinge on their charm. The trick is to quell their unreserved bonhomie long enough to get to their heart and insist that they be "real." Try saying "Stop."

The Hardest Workers Often Have the Lowest Self-Esteem

Want something done? Ask someone who has something to prove.

An inferiority complex has little to do with the situation at hand. One can often trace its roots to a mom or dad who was stingy with approval. When parents refuse to acknowledge their children's feats lovingly, they usually create children who will perform lifetimes of backflips, still hoping to garner that attention. We owe that, the unacknowledged achievement, for the world's workaholic perfectionists.

To someone with an inferiority complex, any obligation can look like a fresh opportunity to wring that withheld approval out of their parents, whom they now carry around in their heads. They can never do enough. Those who never got the nod from their families will give every ounce of strength and then some to make almost anyone's head bob.

The work completed by a person with the inferiority complex may be perfect, but the inferiority still hovers because "Mom and Dad" remain coldly impassive in the bleachers. This is why those who feel inferior do not necessarily please and connect with the people they interact with in the here and now. They are still performing for a hidden audience intrapsychically.

Control Freaks
Secretly Fear Being Out of Control

If someone is being fastidious, will they automatically descend into an ever more hedonistic stupor? Of course not, yet this is the basis of the obsessive-compulsive personality. No one is better defended than people whose own potential for decadence terrifies them.

Witness Felix Unger so longing to blend in with the guys for the card game but endlessly replenishing snacks and disinfecting the kitchen instead. Felix recognizes that his connections to everybody, especially Oscar, are fragile. Fear of abandonment raises his anxiety level and he becomes more controlling to control his anxiety.

Uncontrollable control does drive people away, working against the very outcome the controller often most fears. Don't waste your time trying to *convince* the obsessive-compulsive to relax. They don't know how. I'm not suggesting that you exploit them. However, since they revel in detail-oriented tasks, while not give them a few? When they come up for air, try gently to cajole them into a hot tub, or maybe just a chair.

"People Who Need People" May Be Troubled

This pretty lyric has some less pretty ramifications. People who can't tell up from down without help are what shrinks call dependent personalities. Dependent personalities base their resolve on what other people think is best for them rather than on their own inclinations. They don't say what they really feel. And they're always trawling for caregivers so that they won't have to take care of themselves. Remember *Seinfeld's* George Costanza. He is a textbook-perfect example of a dependent personality.

These people probably weren't born spineless. Their parents' inadequate show of confidence made them this way. They were probably never encouraged to make decisions on their own, and when they did, those decisions were heavily criticized. As a result, they spend their lives trying to rope other people into functioning as the parental backbone they feel they lacked.

Frequently men, in particular, in whom dependency is discouraged, mask their neediness with macho. They will do whatever it takes—bench-press 400 pounds, arm-wrestle a peer into submission—to win the adoration of a woman whom they then expect to tell them what to do. Nor are dependent women slouches at feigning derring-do to snag a man.

Beware. Dependent people cultivate codependency and you'll be a codependent if you play into their neediness. Then you'll need a twelve-step program. You can't cure people who cling, whine, and show little lasting initiative by telling them how, when, and where to stand on their own two feet. They will ultimately resent you, as they do the parent who turned them into such ciphers to begin with. The only way to set a clinger back on his or her own feet is to refuse easy guidance to them, as many times as it takes. Plowing through their anxiety on their own will strengthen their character.

Of course, some people get off by telling others what to do. A coterie of one or more people who hang on their advice may seem to build their own self-worth. By assuming the power of a leading light, the chronic advice giver demonstrates his or her narcissism. When the counsel is self-aggrandizing, the relationship becomes exploitative, as described in the next principle.

What Is on the Outside Is Often the Exact Opposite of What Is on the Inside

Actors and actresses can play confident, healthy characters, but that doesn't always mean they are paragons of emotional health in their real lives. They may be addicts, many times divorced, arrested, etc. Even though most people don't make a profession of deception, nonactors can still cloak their real emotional state. The disguise may fool many or even most people. But shrinks, because it's our job, are constantly on the lookout for signals of depression and other mental disorders.

Here comes a guy with an extra glow, brightening up the day with merriment. Look carefully. All the jocularity may result in what psychiatrists call inappropriate affect. He may even giggle while describing something sad or disturbing. That is a tip-off to a disguised depression. So try to take a second look. Overt expression is not necessarily an accurate meter for emotional health, and quick readings can overlook a lot of pathology.

Displays of either confidence or self-deprecation can also be deceptive. Shyness or boldness. Assertiveness or restraint. Over time, we create and refine some pretty elaborate personas to mask our inner feelings. And the more we practice our routines, the more persuasive they become. These "characters" work because they keep others from identifying our deeper turmoil.

Problem is, outward expressions that belie underlying feelings encumber meaningful growth. That is why it is so important to chisel away at the "act" and expose why it has been cultivated. Is it truly beneficial?

THE INNER SELF

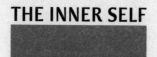

Some People Love to Suffer

They are masochistic. Plain and simple, they seek out grief and are suckers for every tribulation and every passing heartache. We all know such complainers. Every time we hear from them their burden has grown greater and more intolerable. The news is always bad. The "glass" is always almost entirely empty. Yet they go on. And everything continues to go wrong.

Where does the masochistic predilection originate? Sometimes it can be traced to unconscious guilt, the individual feeling that he or she deserves to suffer. They may want what they believe suffering will bring. Unflagging ability to withstand suffering also suggests a sense of moral superiority, a heroic ability to shoulder burdens of increasing magnitude. Maybe we are all a little masochistic. Life has many challenging interludes, more grueling for some than others, and masochism perhaps helps us and our species survive it. It is when the burden feels heavier than the reward, or the anticipated reward, that dyed-in-the-wool masochists identify themselves.

Habitual masochists seem to beg for help, yet they will almost always deny the help when it is there. They want pain. And they want to prove that they will can receive pain . . . and always bear up under it.

Instead of trying to help them overcome their suffering, I have found that it is sometimes more therapeutic to encourage them to suffer more. In other words, you might say, "For the sake of your daughter, please go get examined for your chest pain, even though you know it is a waste of time." You make it sound like they are taking on more suffering, but it's for their own good. It sounds counterintuitive, but when their pleas for acknowledgment of their suffering are met with commendation over their ability to withstand distress, they may very soon lose interest in their suffering and allow themselves to take positive action.

Some People Never Forgive a Favor

Egotists have a grandiose view of themselves in every aspect. Able to outdo everyone, they think they have everything,
do everything, and know everything. Their arrogance may even
be unconscious, though it can come across to people they are
around because they are always condescending. Bigheaded
though they may be, they do welcome help. They love people
groveling after them looking for ways to make them as fabulous
as they already believe they are.

However, an underlying envy pervades every narcissist.
They cannot abide the inference that they may be lacking in any
respect. So they resent it when someone does something for
them that they cannot do for themselves. It goes against their
unreal view of their omnipotence. Accepting a favor feels like
accepting a flaw in their image of themselves. They just can't
do it.

So what do they do? They get even.

Overtly, they may express gratitude, but inwardly they look
for ways to treat the person who has helped them shabbily. If
you know something a narcissist doesn't know, they will, however unconsciously, torture you for it. On the one hand they
take; on the other they may move to "destroy." For the narcissist,
this strategy serves to restore his position at the fulcrum of his
own skewed domain.

Don't Swim with Sharks,
Except in Very Big Pools . . .

Voracious narcissists, though charismatic, have sharp teeth. They lure others into their service if those others have the skills to accentuate their narcissistic success. These predators move forward with their lackeys in tow. However, when anything goes wrong—and something always does—the lackeys get jettisoned. Sharks blame others, never themselves, and they are always the very last of their school to take the blow.

In the competitive workplace, sharks are everywhere. If they recognize your talent, you may benefit from their power, but there is always a price. A few coping principles for surviving the swim:

- Do not try to one-up a shark. They may direct their considerable energy toward destroying you so that they will no longer have to envy you.
- Do not criticize them.
- Do not expect gratitude.
- Do not trust them.
- Do not believe what they say about themselves or about others.
- Do not marry them. (If you have already married a shark, read on.)

. . . Because Vain People Marry Accessories . . .

Remember the Greek Narcissus, a youth of unparalleled beauty who so adored his own reflection that he could not love anyone else? The poor conceited fool ultimately wasted away from unrequited desire. Narcissists characteristically marry other "exalted beings," not because they love them, but to ornament their own excellence. These partners may be either good-looking and submissive, or good-looking and dynamic. Either way, conflicts soon develop because the relationship has shallow foundations.

Narcissists cannot extract the adulation they think they require from a spouse for many reasons. They cannot share. They cannot bear for anyone else to initiate. They do not register other people's feelings. They would rather besmirch anything the spouse does than let attention stray from their own glory. If the spouse is an alter-narcissist with equal greed and guile, the marriage will be explosive.

Knowing narcissists' limitations, the trick is to avoid marrying one out of infatuation. The vain spouse's insistence on control will undermine the partner's attempts to improvise or bring personal aspirations into the relationship. And the narcissist's insistence on adulation is so overbearing that, from his or her perspective, there is no question about who is more righteous. A way to avoid constant anger, one of the biggest challenges, is to distance oneself. The partner shouldn't believe that all the criticism the narcissist levies is merited. This is no small task, and it is very difficult to survive in a marriage wherein all the love is one way.

. . . And the Exploitable Often Cling to the Exploiters

In the shadow of narcissists, dependent people become exploitable people. Commonly, wusses are drawn to narcissists like iron to a magnet, as employees, as friends, as constituents, as lovers and spouses. The egotist exploits his or her groupie, using them to achieve self-aggrandizing goals. And the groupie relies on the egotist for direction, drive, and pride. Since they meet each other's needs, it's near-ideal symbiosis . . . while it lasts.

But the symbiosis is complicated. Almost everyone with low self-esteem is at first flattered by a bigwig's appreciation. However, the consistent lack of nurturing will sooner or later become so glaring that it cannot be denied. Even a doormat eventually finds a just target for rage in the exploitative narcissist.

When the exploited confronts the narcissist, exposing the self-centeredness, one of two events usually transpires. The narcissist will sometimes cast off the "ingrate" and reach out to pull some other weakling into his or her sphere of influence. And without concerted effort, the exploited person will be drawn to a new predator.

Occasionally, narcissists reveal themselves as healthier narcissists. These are those who are relieved if not grateful to be exposed. The exposure makes them feel "understood," and they may even eventually thank their minion for bringing their tendencies to light. This is not necessarily tantamount to correcting the inequality, for it will be difficult for either party to rectify such deep-seated tendencies. Chances are good that after a brief hiatus they will fall back into the familiar superior-inferior relationship.

Excessive Competition
Does Not a Good Bedfellow Make

Highly driven people often botch their personal lives. Though professionally masterful, they just can't seem to cut a deal with a mate. All that swagger, though seductive, can make them unsettling to settle down with because they just can't seem to turn off their desire to triumph, even if it's over their spouse and/or children.

I'm not saying that driven men and women cannot stay hitched; I'm merely pointing out that loving relationships rely on a willingness to make our partners and families our number one priority most of the time. Compulsive winners need to leave their competitive urge on the stoop, and assume their open, receptive, and giving mate-selves once they cross the threshold.

This switch can be particularly challenging for those whose professions demand one-upmanship. The adjustments can make them feel schizophrenic, as they move from cutthroat to romantic. One tip to making this transformation is for competitor types to remember that their families are not, in this regard, an "other," but rather an extension of themselves. They are *on the same team*. And to be fair, it is not entirely up to the competitor alone to switch hats. It takes a compassionate, patient partner to help turn competitors into lovers . . . without killing them first.

Those Who Can't Get Comfortable
in Their Own Skin May Claw at Others . . .

People who cannot accept even a modicum of blame "implant" persecution in others. Their self-righteousness is like impenetrable armor, with a reflective surface on both the exterior and interior. Powerfully destructive, it cultivates paranoia in the self-righteous person and magnifies fault in others. The paranoid then has an enemy—the other guy. And it's certainly a lot easier to combat an external adversary than wage war against oneself internally. That way, the irritation isn't the paranoid's fault; it's someone else's.

As we all know though, paranoia will destroy you. For paranoids, the unconscious longing to establish demons outside, to position them anywhere except in their own head, is unstoppable. Suspiciousness breeds anxiety. Everything that occurs has the potential to become the personal undoing that they deserve but cannot admit to.

Remember Humphrey Bogart's Captain Queeg in *The Caine Mutiny?* Queeg's obsession with his crew's incompetence escalates. Finally, he demands a full account for each and every strawberry on the navy battleship. Queeg's intensifying angst ultimately backfires. He alienates his crew and is relieved of command, and of strawberries.

An inability to accept complicity in one's fate not only results in humiliation; it assures it. Though acknowledgment of weakness, or even need, seems to undermine inner and outer shows of strength, refusal to acknowledge is very often much more destructive.

. . . So Give Paranoids a Wide Berth

Recognizing a paranoid is one skill; dealing with him or her is another. Approach the mistrustful as you would a coiled cobra, by backing up. It sounds counterproductive, I know, but no one appreciates space like a paranoid. The people they trust least are the outgoing types. They fret, "Why is this guy being so nice to me?" Since vague recognition of their own culpability is at their core, paranoids always believe others have an ulterior motive, that they are out to get them. So they react to excessive kindness by tautening with trepidation.

Cool and aloof is what they're after. Hands-off works better than hands-on. The last thing they want is to feel as if they are under someone's thumb, so giving space diminishes conflicts. The wider the zone and the greater the amount of self-control they experience, the more likely that communication and activity will be productive.

Also, fostering independence in a paranoid does the paranoid a favor. It obliges him or her to explore personal capabilities and weigh them against fears that originate inside, not out. His naturally suspicious nature will have to survive on its own juices.

The Dog-Eat-Dog World Cultivates Paranoia

There is destructive paranoia, and then there is *adaptive* paranoia. Adaptive paranoia recognizes real threats and is self-preservationist. Paranoia is adaptive in today's business world where everyone's tail is on the line. As a recent CEO of the Intel Corporation stated, "Only the paranoid survive." The team-player atmosphere is rare these days. It is usually each man for himself. Every move, every encounter has the potential to snafu. Knowing this and operating accordingly is paranoid, but it isn't misplaced paranoia. It's survivalism. The steady anxiety may not be good for your health, but it will put money in the bank.

If your profession has you constantly watching your back, you may need stress management resources if not beta-blockers to keep it from taking a toll. Those not naturally disposed to producing under assault should perhaps seek a less predatory work situation, preferably one with committees or administrators, as groups in general are regressive.

MATURING

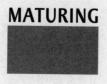

Grown-ups Don't Stop Growing . . .

Your emotional state is not like diabetes. You don't have to be ill for a whole lifetime.

People get healthy at different ages. The term "healthy" is relative and always reflects back to a previous less healthy state. The previous state—the worm-filled fruit of your upbringing—nearly always invites one opportunity after another for paring, paring away its spoiled, malnourishing aspects. Though personal growth is rarely accomplished quickly, the process holds the seeds of growth . . . invariably.

Also "health" is not static. It is not a place that one magically passes into, leaving the unhealthy self behind. First, from an unhealthy state, you see its spark. Then bit by bit you approach it, by trying out new ways of relating to yourself and to the people around you. The pace is often at two steps forward, one backward. It is not unusual for this to take years or even a whole lifetime. Many people go to their grave still totally screwed up. Though this sluggish rate can be, and often is, very disheartening, that is just the way growth is. Growth is a lifelong pursuit.

Once you have that glimmer into your less healthy attributes, and you feel some commitment to overcoming these quirks, you may sometimes feel judgmental and discouraged when you cannot vanquish them easily. Though the feelings are understandable, it is important to remember that just as the damage probably didn't occur overnight, the healing won't either.

Being healthy requires constant tune-ups. Your unhealthy past is like an addictive substance. It sometimes reemerges, a shadow of its former self, to tempt you back to your sicker days. You can engage with it, or turn away from it. Its appearance is like a test, a challenge, or an opportunity to renew your conviction to grow.

. . . But You Can Get Stuck Anywhere, Any Time

This principle gives new meaning to the command "Go to your room!" When parents don't shell out the needed boost to their developing son or daughter at a given age, the child can get stuck at that phase, unable to move on to the next phase, even throughout life. They stay stuck in their room. Psychotherapists know this immobility as arrested development. Here are the classic phases of emotional development:*

Oral Phase (0–18 months)
I am warm, fed, and loved, therefore I feel safe in the world. This phase is called oral because it coincides with the years when a child's most pleasurable stimuli are oral, such as eating, sucking, and biting.

Anal Phase (1–3 years)
I can come and I can go. I can give and I can take. This phase is called anal because it coincides with the years when a child's gratification stems from the ability to retain and excrete feces at will.

Oedipal Phase (3–6 years)
There is both good and bad in me. My desire for sex is good but has to be controlled. My desires to compete and retaliate

---

* These are explained in greater depth in Dr. Colarusso's works, including *Fulfillment in Adulthood*. See bibliography.

against people who hurt me are also good things, but also have to be controlled. When I grow up, I want to be just like Mom (or Dad).

Latency Phase (6–12 years)

I am a girl (or boy) and this is what I do. You are a boy (or girl) and this is what you do. My place in the future lies outside the home and I need to make friends to succeed in the world outside my family.

Adolescent Phase (12–20 years)

I am no longer a child, but a grown-up, and I want sex. I don't want to be just like Mom and Dad; I want to go my own way. I understand that I will have to work for a living and I have some realistic ideas of the broad areas in which I am strongest. I know who I am.

Young Adulthood (20–40 years)

I need to be close to someone. I need to be successful in the workplace. I need to have involvement with youth either as a parent or in some other capacity.

Middle Adulthood (40–60 years)

No longer young, I am engaged in a race against time. I must maximize my potential now as a legacy to the next generation.

Late Adulthood (60+ years)

I need to stay connected to life by maintaining my ties to youth. I need to prepare myself for my inevitable death and come to peace with my life and whatever philosophy helps me to understand death.

Destablized Security Exposes People's Psychological Well-Being

It is relatively easy to stay on course as long as life is going our way. It is when fate throws us an ill wind that we can demonstrate our emotional health.

With their feelings dashed and in smithereens, those who have been devastated may drift aimlessly. They have no internal moorings. They can neither locate nor recognize safe harbor. Ravaged, they are not particularly adept at rafting-up even when opportunity for security is staring them in the face. What they really need is a lifeline, stability imposed on them by others, and they need it desperately. However, by stability I do not mean restraint. I mean structure.

Structure means arbitrary routines—clear guidelines with clear consequences for appropriate and inappropriate behavior. Like boot camp. Just as children need expectations imposed on them, so do people who are emotionally drowning. Likely, they did not benefit from structure as children so they never mastered techniques for navigating out of uncharted waters and foul weather. Suggesting regular disciplines such as exercise and journal keeping can lend them a compass.

As We Age, No One Escapes the
Consequences of Uncompleted Work . . .

If life is like a river, the aforementioned phases of emotional development are like eddies. We get caught up in their lessons for as long as it takes to gather strength to plunge onward, with momentum, to the next eddy. Our ability to experience each phase fully and then move on depends partially on people and exposures that either aid or hinder us. Those emotional tasks which we do not complete reappear, and we continue to either work through them or not. Each phase is more challenging than the one before because it demands that we employ everything we have already learned in order to accomplish and integrate new challenges. Obviously, no law says we have to move on beyond our current ability. Though sometimes staying stuck in a phase can hurt us and others who love us.

For example, a man may have trouble getting married because earlier in his life during his Oedipus years he already unconsciously "married" his overinvolved mother. It may be that he fears marriage because he does not want to become his hypercritical father. Although this reluctant adult passed through subsequent phases—the latency and adolescent periods—he gets bogged to a standstill in young adulthood because his parents did not sufficiently support the transition through the Oedipal phase.

People who want to move beyond blockage—and that does not include everyone—need to recognize where they became snagged and provide themselves with what their parents could not: good motivations for moving on.

. . . Therefore, the Most Important Element of Mildlife Transition Is Honesty

The problem with midlife is that, like a fungus, it creeps up on you. There is plenty of time to deny that you are aging, plenty of time to stave off the inevitable. A fountain of youth regimen can help fool the world into believing you are still a whippersnapper, but it can become too easy to fool yourself as well. This can't go on forever. Time marches forward.

Midlife has its own opportunities, too often ignored by our culture and by the very people who should be its connoisseurs—the middle-aged. It is a plateau, a place of experience, with a view of the past that can be far more realistic and better informed from a forty- or fifty-something vantage point. It is normal, honest, and productive to acknowledge irrevocable life decisions during middle age, to become aware of your mortality. This awareness leads to introspection and usually some melancholy. The passage may be uncomfortable, but honesty is essential. Middle-aged people are ideally positioned to review and reassess, and then make decisions about how to progress. Yes, *progress!* Midlife is not the end. It is the middle.

Time to jettison any emotional lodestones that disserved you. Adulthood's first half is ideal for examining and overcoming childhood problems such as inadequate parenting. Half a century is years enough to be a kid. Perhaps time to let go of some of those self-serving goals too, to move toward broader-minded objectives. In truth, trivial egocentric activities that absorbed a midlifer's previous attention are no longer satisfying. With fewer years ahead, they can create new demands for themselves—to spend their talents on more universally rewarding pursuits that will leave a legacy to their loved ones and communities. This makes midlife a time of fulfillment and builds a foundation that they will look back upon with pride as they move toward the end of their lives.

Men Throw Reason Out the Window During a Midlife Crisis (That's Why It's Called a *Crisis*)

Is a fifty-something man really more sexually desirable than a twenty-something stud? Practically never, unless the woman has father issues. Is embarking on a liaison with a woman half one's age going to prevent a man from aging? Of course not. Is a woman who would allow her financial needs and insecurity to break up a family really lovable? Not entirely. Do any of these evident inequities trouble the man who is hell-bent on resurrecting his potency? No.

That is the kernel of the midlife crisis. No amount of logic can awaken the man who refuses to look his declining years in the face. Even a modicum of encouragement from a younger woman is enough to send him into a delusional reverie. *The chemistry. The intrigue. The sex. The novelty!* Only if he says he has never felt so alive is he even partially accurate. He hasn't felt alive because his emotions may have been on the snooze cycle for the last thirty years.

If this is true—and it often is in such cases—the midlife crisis may be a departure point for change. It's about turning the reverie to revelry. Wake-up time.

If he doesn't accept reality right now, he's going to wake up hungover and alone in a place far from home six months later, asking himself what he has done. In a culture that worships youth, no one looks forward to becoming a geezer. But a more comprehensive understanding of aging bestows a more rewarding fate. What about wisdom? What about perspective? What about loyalty? Men of any age, and women too for that matter, need to reassess their values, to weigh what is most important. Is it more important to get or to give? The broadened perspective afforded by advancing years makes this reassessment easier, as long as fear of aging and death does not overwhelm.

Being a Grandparent
May Be Life's Greatest Pleasure

No one is better qualified to determine life's happiest moments than those who have most sampled life's offerings—the AARP set.

As the end of a life richly lived approaches, what could be more uplifting to behold than the medley of your family's DNA? No matter your belief system, recognizing the legacy of your genetic imprint helps give life meaning—and at a phase during which making sense of it all is most important. Aside from the intrinsic joy of interacting with young people, playing and talking with grandchildren is an excursion back in time. It glimmers with memories of the grandparent's every previous phase. You, the grandparent, reexperience some of the moments you had with your own children. Time has worked miracles on those memories, deepening the exquisite parts and dulling the difficulties. The activities take you even farther back in time, back to your own childhood, to the activities you still remember, to the trials that seemed so inordinate then, upon which you can only smile presently.

You picture your grandchild's future, and it seems to have all the promise of your own maturation, only more so. And spending time with a grandchild, you have the opportunity to impart added bequest—doling out the wisdom, assets, good deeds, and cookies.

Being a grandparent is life's most tangible way of "living on" and redoubles the rewards of parenting—life's other greatest pleasure.

People Who Deal Well with Life,
Deal Well with Death

Evidently, neuroses, addictions, abusive behavior, and other emotionally based problems do not occur when people are at ease with the hand they have been dealt. These behaviors are painful and pain-causing expressions of dispiritedness. When faced with death, troubled individuals are also faced with their own failure to redress that dealt hand. This situation compounds their anger and dread. Then a sort of psychological mayhem occurs, intensified by the separation and irrevocability of mortality.

This internal clash—which is usually externalized—might be over the expiration of a loved one or even an enemy, or it might be over that person's own impending death. Anyone's death rattles the foundations and causes us to look more critically at our picayune daily preoccupations.

As oncologists and other physicians know only too well, illness is a great if torturous teacher, and those who are passed a death sentence become pupils in a new chapter of life, whether willing or otherwise.

Many people, indeed most people, spend their entire lives trying to skirt the inevitability of the lessons. Their efforts may be as prosaic as an unwillingness to honor their own aging and a dogged pursuit of longevity. They may also have a more ambitious quest for "immortality," whether through creativity or fame. Commonly, a dying person may be moody, crotchety, and downright mean. Of course, none of these manifestations keeps the bitter end at bay, but they are profound expressions of the person's link with life.

This is not to criticize anyone's apprehension about death, particularly as none of us knows how we ourselves will act when it is our turn. Death is "the unknown," and dealing with the unknown gracefully is perhaps life's greatest challenge.

PARENTING

Parenthood Is Life's Most Rewarding Classroom

The needs of a growing, developing child pull, and sometimes force, parents, grandparents, and other caregivers out of their shell. Even people who have never had their own children, but who at some point in their lives involve themselves in a parental role, reap many uplifting rewards from the efforts. Children enrich our lives and draw us away from self-centeredness. Ask any new parent or anyone newly involved in a child's life for any reason; as is evident by their love-filled blithering, it is an experience that defies description.

Sometimes, inadvertently, children take charge of teaching. Adults find themselves in a school of their children's creation—learning new lessons, much beyond the awesome challenges of sleepless nights and diaper changing. Humility. Bravery. Tenacity. Compassion. Responsibility. Patience . . . just to name a few. All are lessons our parents tried to teach us, but we didn't "get" them until we matriculated in the School of Parenthood. Children teach us to see life in a whole new way, and it's plentiful.

Children never cease being children. Though the nuts and bolts of parenting change as kids mature, they still need nurturing. They need attention. They need listening. They need interaction. All this "need" may suggest an open vein on a parent or caregiver's part, but not necessarily, because the exchange is its own reward.

No matter what your children say to you, they still need you.

And you, if you're honest, need them. The faulty thinking is that we stop parenting when our kids grow up. But it just isn't so. We never stop taking care of our children until the day we die. The ties are too strong. And they will carry on their love and the memory of our love far longer than that.

Supermom Is As Real As Superman

In the olden days Mom simply had eyes in the back of her head. Today, Mom is new and improved. She jets from dinner dishes to sex to bagged lunches to office to meetings to soccer practice and back to dinner dishes, often whipping up bake sale cupcakes while putting the finishing touches on a corporate takeover before she's back in the sack with Dad. Plus, she's beautiful. And nice. And smart. And understanding. Turbomama's too good to believe.

That's because she doesn't exist. This superheroine is the product of overambitious feminism on a planet where men will be men. Even though women are master multitaskers, and the second set of eyes is still there, no woman can or should try to be everything to everyone, at least not without a cape and some swell lasers.

Each woman needs to make individual decisions, consciously, about her priorities. Time constraints are especially a factor in her children's early years. Does she want to be there for her children herself? Or can she relinquish some caregiving, or parenthood itself, if her career offers her more gratification? She needs to recognize that guilt she feels about the decision to work may be irrational, because it is impossible to "do it all."

Women and families have done a terrific job of bending rules that originated in the *Father Knows Best* years. The workplace has accommodated the changes with opportunities for job-sharing, home offices, and better daycare. Moreover, technology has made both parenting and work physically easier. In exchange, there is more homework and more child-moving—driving little darlings, with their (hopefully) appended backpacks and other accoutrements, between school, extracurricular activities, and friends' houses—the price of living in a world with less open space and more danger. Frenetic, this pace takes a different sort of exhaustive toll.

So, the working-mom agenda can be very taxing. When it gets too overwhelming, it is Mom's job to stop changing identities at every phone booth. By making tough decisions about priorities, she'll wind up casting off a few of her alter egos. Then, though the decisions will be a compromise, she needs to accept them without guilt. And her family, particularly her husband, needs to accept them without recrimination.

Good Parenting Is Founded on Consistency

All children internalize their parenting, carrying Mom and Dad around like invisible extra brains for the rest of their lives. How their parents relate to them is how they come to relate to themselves, as well as the way they react to the outside world.

To a child, life is an unknown. A child has no way of knowing life's potential or its boundaries. The mystery of life must be revealed in controlled, digestible amounts, a little bit at a time, so the child can slowly establish who he or she is from a point of safety. Without a sense of security, fear may misdirect the child's actions in very unpredictable and unfortunate ways. This is why it is imperative that parents impart consistent routines, consistent rewards, and consistent punishments. Without consistency, a child has no anchor. He or she will constantly test, looking for the resistance that will define boundaries, asking for stability.

Imagine the terror of an astronaut, having lost his connection to his craft and to Earth, adrift in space. Irrational behavior in such a situation would not be surprising. Nor is it surprising in an unanchored child. Inconsistent limit setting leads to impulsive, demanding children, ricocheting through life to see how far they can go. *No* will never mean no. It will always mean maybe.

For the rest of their lives, they will have difficulty accepting any sort of restriction. They will push for immediate gratification, no matter the consequences. And when they get what they want, they will ask for more. Each request repeats the original desire for their parents to tether them.

Don't confuse indulgence with love. It will be mortifying to claim credit for children whose temperament is such that their peers spurn them. If spoiled children can, as adults, avoid incarceration, they may become warlords, despised by their minions. The fate of the earth is on parents' shoulders. Wouldn't it be better to let *no* mean no?

If You Drag Your Children Back to Eden, Forbidden Fruit Will Be a Bumper Crop

Some parents traipse around in the altogether, disregarding the importance of appearing clothed in front of their children. Bare-bottomed moms and dads would perhaps not be such a big deal if the yearning for sex did not gather momentum like a cyclotron as children mature and reach adolescence. When the urge reaches atom-splitting force, no amount of well-intended back-to-nature logic is going to help a teenager separate Mom's and Dad's body parts from parental nurturing. The hormone-laced teenage years are already an emotional jungle. Why hang them with familial genitals too? Your sons and daughters will have plenty to overcome just by taking care of the erupting sensations between their own legs.

You're just pulling on clothes, not wool over your children's eyes. Kids numbly acknowledge that their parents are equipped to have sex. That's why there is sexual tension between parents and children. But it is most healthful if that awareness is not too near the surface. Otherwise, developing teens may have to do anything to ward off forbidden desires for their parents. They may have sex willy-nilly, frequently, and with just about anyone, to parry the longing for the parent. Or they may shut down sexually and emotionally, throwing their longing behind the chastity belt in what shrinks call repression of sexuality.

If either of these extremes were transitory, the effect of the parents' lack of sexual discretion and boundaries might not be so dramatic. But not so. Unfortunately, whatever they do to compensate for sexual tension in the family usually continues and can blight their adult sex lives. Knowing that every child-parent relationship is somewhat incestuous, isn't it worth a little modesty?

The Children of Overprotective Parents Become Underprotected Adults

The world is a minefield, granted. It's not like the good old days when children could crawl unattended through the neighborhood safely. But parents who worry disproportionately and out loud over the abundant hazards that confront their children bequeath a legacy of angst. Their heirs will divvy the bad bounty into any number of neurotic behaviors. All children stash a memory of Mom and Dad within them for a lifetime. But these kids' internalized mom or dad will not be a comfort to them; it will sound like a siren and feel like a porcupine.

Children who lack this core nurturing try to extract it from elsewhere, unrelentingly, by whatever means works. Some become model exhibitors of separation anxiety. Throughout their lives they hold others hostage with their behaviors as they continually reach to extract the reinforcement they never had from their parents.

Alternatively, anxious kids frequently develop what's known as a counterphobic lifestyle of risk taking, rebellion, and substance abuse. This rebellion is a way of trying out the dark imaginings seeded by their parents, of proving that Mom and/or Dad were mistaken about their fragility.

Warm reassurance, on the other hand, imparts a message of loving confidence in a child, and works to cultivate the child's eventual self-stewarding. Given society's growing array of dangers, the challenge to parents is ever greater. But children normally seek and require greater degrees of responsibility and confidence as they grow. If the love and assurance can be imparted, as the child matures, he or she carries the memory of this original velvet-glove security. It will help him or her actualize a fulfilling life and maneuver out of life's tight places.

Don't Be Adolescent in Dealing with Adolescents

We all have a little residual teenager in us—explosive reactions, untempered emotions, and even occasional acne. For most adults, these tendencies remain checked as long as we're in control (as we are when dealing with younger children), or as long as we're dealing with reasonable adults. A teenager, who may be big enough to look directly in the eye, or even bigger, often can't be controlled and won't be reasonable. They're souped up on hormones. Hence, in exasperation, parents dealing with their teenagers sometimes find themselves overcome by a fury they haven't felt for thirty-odd years . . . and acting it out!

Further, children's teen years coincide with their parents' midlife. The adults have their noses pressed uncomfortably against their remaining years. Their own parents are growing enfeebled and dying. That's a blow, and though common, it is not an easy place to be. Without their own parents to help them, adults may feel, however unconsciously, up a creek without a paddle.

Plus, by the time kids reach the double digits they are fully equipped to operate every function on their parents' control panel. The results can be volatile, with everyone—regardless of age—screaming, throwing things, and slamming doors. At best, it's a sitcom. At worst, it's a mess.

It isn't easy to keep cool when teenagers behave provocatively. But here's the rub: The parent whose reaction is hotheaded is playing by the teenager's rules. And worse: The teen, having driven the parent to apoplexy, may feel vindicated in his original outburst. Nothing is resolved; in fact, things are worse. Pass the oxybenzene.

Be aware of the sexual tension too. In experiencing their own exploding sexuality, most teens feel compelled to pull away from sexual feelings for their parents. Friction and door slamming are a way of creating distance if nothing else works.

In stepfamilies the teen interval can become even more problematic, with everyone involved repressing misplaced sexual urges. It isn't easy for any man to deal gracefully with bodacious sixteen-year-olds with bare navels and tight clothing, much less a stepfather. Or how about a stepmother eyeing the broad-shouldered virility of a high school athlete who is likely a younger version of the man she married, only without the paunch? An effective way to master the situation is to recognize that these are natural but unacceptable temptations. The teen years demand greater distance for good reasons.

The best approach is to respect your teen's need for detachment and autonomy. Part of this is encouraging him or her to express feelings and interests and to listen with respect, not judgment. Ask questions. Try to establish a relationship. The fewer issues that are bottled up, the less likely there will be an eruption.

Kids Need Both Parents

Children need to establish their own relationship with both their mothers and their fathers. This is just as true of divorced parents as of married parents. Only if a parent is abusive should the child be denied this opportunity. The reason for this is clear. Parents—good or bad—are a child's touchstone for all events that follow in his or her life. In addition to the valuable history about the child's origins that parents provide, moms and dads also become emblems that define a child's experience of gender. This includes informing, through the unconscious, all intimate relations of their adolescence and adulthood. And the relationship with both parents also gives them a point of departure for defining their own way of parenting, should that occur.

The idea that one can be both father and mother to a child can stretch only so far. Yes, some families have no choice. But often acrimonious relations between divorced parents put unnecessary limits on the child's exposure to either the father or the mother. The custodial parent self-righteously justifies the limitation as being in the child's best interests. This justification robs the child in many ways. Further, in the space where a memory of a parent should be there is a big zilch. The child will never know the parent, unless he or she pursues the relationship as an adult, and the child won't benefit from the gender references that the parent might have provided.

In still-married households too, it is rewarding for parents to spend time alone with each child occasionally, without the other parent. Excursions, throwing the ball, reading, talking, and just relating with one parent at a time—these are pastimes that build a repertory of memories in a child. They will teach him or her what bonding is and what love is capable of.

Mothers' Primal Bond Is, First and Foremost, to Their Children

That's why moms get rabid at PTA meetings and disappear into flaming buildings to rescue their budding pyromaniacs. No woman is going to abandon a connection to someone who once fit inside her like an extra organ, at least not usually. And any man who forgets this is asking for a headache. Mothers' bonds with their children don't have anything to do with men. There are great reasons for this, reasons having to do with perpetuation of the species. When men challenge this, conflict results. The object of his affection turns into a she-wolf.

A man who is narcissistic or insecure can resent the nurturing his spouse or lover showers on her child. He may vie with the kid for attention. He may even attempt to force the woman to make choices that favor him over the child. This is neither noble nor thought through. What sort of man would want a woman who would desert vulnerable children for an adult?

Once there is a child in the picture, the situation is not "about" the grown-ups. It's not a case of one partner's priorities winning out over the other partner's. The two-human league becomes something grander and more complex—a family—and the adults must make decisions that work best, not just for one or the other of them, but for everybody under the umbrella, especially in children who don't yet know when to come in from the rain.

This can get challenging in stepfamilies, where issues of

guilt, abandonment, anger, and low self-esteem regularly roil like unsettled waters. But it is not impossible, if the adults are adult.

The sooner men wise up about the inviolable nature of the maternal tether, the sooner they'll gather more real influence. A woman's feelings for her mate strengthen when he invests in her child or children's well-being. She has a tough job and she needs help. It's that simple.

This same principle cuts two ways, particularly these days with men assuming stronger parenting roles. A new wife may resent her husband's affection for children from his previous marriage. But this commitment to his progeny is a reflection of a responsible and dedicated man. Perhaps she should be happy to have snagged such a prize!

In a Divorce, Children Often Lose

Children of divorcing parents regularly become hostages of their parents' egos and attitudes about money. Mothers and fathers can insist on more custody, sometimes claiming that they really want to spend time with their children. Very often the real reason, however unexpressed, is that more time equals less financial support and more pain to the other spouse—and thus feeds divorce's dishonorable dual objective. That's how children get split in ways that aren't supported by love. Throw in bitterness between the parents, and especially a parent who degrades the other parent in front of kids, and it's a raw deal that can do unquantifiable damage to the children.

Adults who use their children as pawns in a different but persisting war have not really severed their negative involvement with their ex-spouses. They continue to spar, now not just at their expense, but at their children's. Not only does their action hurt children in the moment, it also inculcates them with deep resentment toward the very people they want most to trust.

Adults choose each other, before they have children, and they need to remember that that choice is their responsibility. Hapless offspring, who have no choice, shouldn't have to shoulder the burden of someone else's bad decision. In a psychological climate that scorns the idea of staying together for the sake of the children, this may be misperceived as a rebel view. But I maintain that children need advocacy.

Children change everything in terms of how one contemplates the decision to stay or leave. Unless marriages are abusive, parents should shake off their solipsism. Lack of perfect compatibility is a dumb reason for divorce. No couples are one hundred percent compatible. The grass simply is greener on the other side of the hill, but at some point you choose your hill and its turf. Personal work, which doesn't treat the family like grounded passengers with guns to their head, can revolutionize the situation dramatically, hurting no one.

Mental Health Problems Can Suddenly Surface During Adolescence

Who hasn't heard of the angelic child who, once the hormones kick in, throws off the halo? The teen dislodges a full repertory of psychological disturbances that jar the family like rounds from an AK-47. Abruptly becoming detainees of a newly hatched terrorist, parents wring their hands in bewilderment, fretting, "What happened to my perfect child?"

People excuse teenagers a lot. It's the habit of parents who receive the jolt of the teenage years unawares to be defensive. Sure, adolescence is a self-defining time, a time for identifying who one is apart from being a child, apart from the family. But the span is not necessarily annihilative—to either oneself or others—unless there are underlying reasons for anger.

Teenage years turn up the volume. Quiet, heretofore unexpressed issues begin to surface, first in bumpy disquietude, then—if no one pays any attention—at full jarring intensity. Kids who have appeared perfectly normal and well adjusted sometimes wait until their teens to stage crises they've felt and borne internally for years.

There are always sources of bad or troubled behavior. A careful analysis, which looks in depth, finds earlier indications. *Come to think of it, he never really had a relationship with his father . . . or She was really very quiet and to herself . . . or He never wanted to play with children his own age.*

To distinguish ordinary adolescent problems from extraordinary ones, parents can apply the clinical rule of thumb: Can the maturing child work and love? When the jungle of the teenage years interferes with school performance and affectionate relationships, something is wrong. This is what shrinks call functional impairment. Teen suicide has become too serious an issue for parents or anyone else to trivialize a teen's signs that he or she is depressed.

Importantly, parents should not disregard or deny what is occurring. Their child's behavior and attitude may be the harbinger of a genetic time bomb like schizophrenia or of a drug problem. But more likely they have everyday issues that must be dealt with now. That teenagers find a way to express feelings that they've buried throughout their childhood may be for the good. Why keep all that bottled up?

The problems are most often rooted in fear over the formidable challenges of self-sufficiency in the young adulthood that yawns before them. Critically, it is incumbent on parents to recognize this. Kids seek confidence in their adultness in order to cope with these anxieties. Therefore, parents need to avoid treating them in a condescending, authoritarian way that undermines their belief in themselves.

There Is Passion in Family Life

What is passion? It is a heart that soars in recognition of its object. A wonderment at life's treasures. A gradual building of mutual adoration. Shared awareness. Common objectives. Overcoming obstacles together. *It is connection.*

Family life is too often trivialized when compared to the first flush of romance couples feel as infatuation. But the family has, by the very people who are involved in it—your loved ones—more potential for enduring rapture than any other connection.

Hold your child in view. Your child is a magic carpet ride. You can, on the threads of his or her imagination and potential, visit the most distant corners of bliss. Your child's maturation will not be without challenges. But these challenges need not dilute your devotion; they can fortify it as working together to overcome them increases your intimacy. Interaction and exchange with your child builds a bastion of love that will be your ultimate expression on this planet.

This excursion is unique to each parent. The private moments, sustained in memory, are an exquisite pleasure. Sharing the experience with others who love the child too—be they the other parent, grandparents, stepparents, or siblings—makes the construct, the passion of family life, that much more vivid and broadens the passion to include more individuals.

ISSUES OF DESPAIR

Hopelessness Is Emotional Cyanide

Despair, like a millstone, can drag people into immobility. They can't work. They can't take care of themselves. They can't take care of others. Once productive pursuit is eliminated, inactivity lets the mind chew on itself, viewing and reviewing an expanding repertory of lousy feelings. As people who have been seriously depressed know, this spiraling descent into hopelessness is powerfully destructive. It can be fatal. It's the worst and most terrifying enemy most of us ever have to encounter. And because the enemy is invisible, yet entirely encompassing, it is difficult to resist or combat.

Labeling hopelessness as the enemy is the first counteroffensive. This can give people distance from depression, because "it" then has an identity. They can come to distinguish the sentiments of despair as they occur. Once it is recognizable, hopelessness is not so pervasive; it has its own boundaries like a separate country.

Then, patients must engage hopelessness in battle as if it were Satan himself. It's a war, not a skirmish. They can, either on their own or with professional help, develop a combat strategy and start implementing its tactics. The short-term tactic is distraction, to force thoughts away from succumbing to the lethal hopelessness. Effective distractions are different for everyone. One person must get outside. Another should read. Exercise. Meditate. There are many options, but activity is essential. Get out that calendar and jam it with pursuits.

The force of hopelessness will attempt to bleed enthusiasm from these distractions and there is a tendency to trivialize their worth. But distractions, by their very nature, have the ability to focus the mind elsewhere, even demand that it go elsewhere. And these short-term approaches may naturally suggest another more challenging involvement that will, if cultivated, grow into passion. Passion is the all-encompassing opposite of hopelessness.

Nurture Cannot Always Overcome Nature

Sometimes, chemical imbalance, brought about by genes, disease, environment, or trauma, can send emotions into a descent so swift that no amount of love or therapy can buoy it. This is no one's fault. It just is. It used to be that those who suffered from these invisible sicknesses were too easily lost. Happily, we can now save minds and lives with psychopharmaceuticals. Thanks to medical ingenuity, we have great little pills that help us put forward our least-fraught thoughts first. Antidepressants, antipsychotics, and mood stabilizers can alleviate the insurmountable burden of chemical imbalance for long enough to sort through the issues that bear changing.

Meds can't fix everything, of course. They can't provide healthy relationships. They can't bring back loved ones who have died. They can't make physical illness disappear. They won't impart a sense of identity or deeper insight. They can't give meaning to life. In short, they can't do the work for you.

However, meds can give you the space—by loosening your mind from debilitating negativity, obsessions, and anxiety—to make these improvements for yourself. The commitment to improve has to be there in a potency that can overcome any inertia depression has brought on. It has been my experience that the healing process is faster and more effective if accompanied by psychotherapy.

People who feel trapped in a biologically based depression sometimes search for reasons to feel bad, reinforcing what they know or have learned about their condition with negatively biased impressions about their lives. For example, a person who comes from a family in which depression has been a problem may shirk personal responsibility for their crummy emotional inheritance. This makes their depression make sense, but it can also be self-deceptive and allows them to cast off the duty only they can perform, that of "getting it together." In a time when psychopharmaceuticals can be so helpful, depression is often completely avoidable. By undoing the biological basis through drug treatment, the person will then be freer to evaluate life changes.

Depression Is the Common Cold of Psychiatry

As ubiquitous as sneezing, depression can overtake just about anyone. It can come from tragedy, from failure, from disease, and from just plain bad body chemistry. Let's face it: There are plenty of reasons to be glum. The challenge is to move through the depression to an awareness that encompasses circumstances outside those that brought on the terrible despondency.

In the last twelve years, the ready availability of new antidepressants and the accompanying media exposure has raised public awareness of depression. Even people who might never have sought psychiatric treatment now have a name for what ails them—*depression*.

Depression occurs in at least three different dynamics. People in the first category are chronically depressed. This means that no matter how light the undertow, they will still be bottomlessly unhappy. Depression is built into them and may be passed from generation to generation. Depressives with this affliction, though substantially more rare, cannot be helped *except* by antidepressants, in my experience. In these cases, psychotherapy may be of little help and a poor use of time and money.

The second dynamic concerns lasting grief that occurs after a severe loss. Its severity is entirely subjective but might occur with the loss of a child, spouse, or loved one, an amputation, mastectomy, a sizable career setback, or loss of functioning brought about by disease or trauma. Time helps, as does an involved other person who listens to the aggrieved as he or she gives words to the pain. This need not be a therapist, but if there is not a strong support system, treatment is very necessary.

The third dynamic involves loss accompanied by anger. People who have unresolved issues with a departed loved one often do not know that they are angry. This despair can set in after messy divorces or after a close relative or friend dies. Since they are not able to storm through these problems by interacting with the object of their anger, they take their antagonism out on themselves instead. Only a strong guide can help people in this third category move toward slow recognition and safe expression of their real feelings. This is usually the only path out of melancholy.

Loss is the common element in all three dynamics. It could be a loss of time, an object, an idealization of an object, or a person. As a result, the therapeutic path always has the same objective—awareness of what one still possesses and takes for granted together with an active search to replace what is missing. It is like the Talmud aphorism about he who is happy being he who is satisfied with what he has. I would add, *And searches for what he wants.*

A Depressed Degenerate Is in Better Shape Than One Who Is Not

Rotten eggs who feel no remorse are usually unreachable. If they are in prison, they should stay there. On the other hand, criminals and other wrongdoers who feel depressed are more likely to have a conscience. And that conscience is a good prognostic handle for reaching them and helping them heal.

The conscience makes a kind of island in the depraved ocean of their usual sentiment. This island provides a specific territory, however difficult to access, that therapists can land on and colonize with remedial work. Psychopharmaceuticals can be helpful in first alleviating the depression, which may have rendered the person entirely inert. With drugs, the depression will subside into ordinary sadness. Once mobilized, the one fallen from grace can better apprehend what has been lost.

From here, the individual may be able to distinguish that even as the world is both bad and good, so is he, or so is she. This contrast, in and of itself, presents the dissolute person with a choice, whereas before this realization there was none. Recognition of the specific loss helps direct a search to replace what is missing or move to counterbalance the loss with constructive "good" action. A therapist may be able to shape this point of view.

This is a significant step toward rehabilitation that can never occur in those who refuse to accept their guilt. The process of rebuilding a psyche with constructive action and relationships works as it does for others, but it usually requires a lot more support and structure for felons.

Castration Anxiety Is Real

If you don't believe me, mention castration and watch men clam up and cross their legs. The core fear of castration is evolutionarily adaptive and emotionally important: Men without genitalia cannot father children.

Castration anxiety stems from childhood. In psychiatric terms, the feared punishment for having sex with your opposite-sex parent is that your same-sex parent will make off with your genitals.

Residually, a boy's fear of being turned into a soprano can lead directly to a fear of success as an adult man. A female correlative of this issue is still extremely controversial. A female's less obvious sexual apparatus is perhaps more difficult to comprehend. The core conflict is the same though. Succeeding, on an unconscious level, might mean one must take the place of the same-sex parent with all its threatening ramifications.

Castration is a broader theme when not taken literally. Any time a human being is denied potency, denied the ability to produce, he or she suffers humiliation. This shame resonates within, amplifying anxiety and undermining efforts to achieve.

When parents encourage their children, letting them know that they perform well, sometimes as well as or better than they themselves do, it helps children overwhelm these castration anxiety demons later in life. It bolsters individuals' confidence, giving them tools and experiences to support their own potency.

People who missed out on this supportive upbringing must, as adults, consciously devote themselves to fortifying their own ego and celebrating their productivity. Lacking the nurturing childhood experience, they must create their own nurturing adult web of positive relationship experiences.

People Regress to Earlier Behaviors Under Stress

Want to see adults act like toddlers? Watch what happens at the scene of an automobile accident, especially if the cars are new and expensive. Or witness the tightly wound person who is trying to get out the door for a major presentation. Whoops! Coffee stains. Lost keys. Bad hair. These seemingly inadvertent delays have much in common with displays of childhood separation anxiety. The presentation itself may look a lot like the competitive Oedipus complex at tilt on a playground, if the presenter is insecure about his or her ability. Or how about the medical ethics committee that spends three or more hours, *anal* hours, dawdling over inconsequential topics instead of coming to a decision about the lascivious Dr. Jones's hospital privileges? Perhaps personal struggles with similar impulses or feelings of betrayal make them act just like four-year-olds. All examples of regression fueled by stress.

Though it sounds and is childish, acting like a kid, albeit unconsciously, is very common. The more stress, the more opportunity to regress. Of course, why should fear and rage evaporate with adulthood? They don't. They just transmute into less explicit expression as people learn to control their emotions.

However, constantly internalizing anxiety may loose free radicals on a cancer-making field day, so it's sometimes more healthful to regress. Shrinks call this wholesome regression a regression in the service of ego. It's really just carte blanche to raise hell, at least once in a while.

To Succeed, Confront Your Fears

For many people, faceless demons continually thwart progress. We don't know why we're trumped up, but we are. Truthfully, it isn't the other guy who makes us fail. It isn't inability that makes us fail. It isn't even fate that makes us fail. *It's fear.* Fear is most people's biggest foe, hobbling forward movement and robbing lives of meaning. No one wants to admit they are petrified, especially by something as familiar as their own potential. Yet fear remains an unassailable enemy until we admit that it exists.

Many will bungle every effort to succeed rather than give up that familiar feebleness that keeps them childlike and insecure. Or worse. People will take the path of least resistance and waste themselves in half-lived lives, all because on some level they realize that any effort to pursue their dreams will put them in touch with what they cannot stand to confront.

Anything can seem preferable to revisiting childhood taunts like "fraidy cat" or the voices of childhood caregivers who continually cajoled us to "grow up." However, the irony is that though we hold our dreams in abeyance, our fear still follows us like a shadow.

When people turn around to get a good gander at their fear—any fear—they gain power. They *know* their enemy. An honest look at the force that has been sucking power from their achievement very often neutralizes the fear's ability to take a toll. The fear may not go away, but it is no longer in control.

People Who Fall Apart over Trivial Matters
May Need Help

Those who have a cow over nothing are part of a less healthy herd. The more generalized their anxiety, the greater is the likelihood of deep-seated unpleasantness that has not been properly sorted through with therapy or some other means, or handled through medication. Underlying loneliness, inadequacy, or shame prompts feelings of apprehension that are protean in their manifestations. Anxiety might range from vague disquietude or phobia to full-blown panic attacks. Peer under the conscious corners of these symptoms and you may find a hotbed of sexual conflict or aggression as the unconscious cause.

The trick to treating anxiety is in letting the deeper issues emerge at a tolerable speed. From the patient's point of view, this increases the sense of safety and self-confidence. Some overly anxious people are pressure cookers, trembling and hissing as sealed-off feelings steam away. Naturally, a slowly opened pressure cooker is less likely to burn. The first step is to persuade the anxious person to acknowledge their real fear of what is inside the cooker, not out.

After that, explore the fear's source—often buried antagonism, but from what? An exploration of such nature will alleviate some of the stress. Usually this is best undertaken in a calm nonjudgmental but inquisitive atmosphere such as cognitive therapy, away from the anxiety's source. Remember the essential harmlessness of experiencing emotion and fantasy. Privately aired thoughts are less likely to become unconscious acts of aggression or conscious anxious misery.

There is a sizable chasm between *experiencing* anxiety and *acting* on anxiety, the latter response being the less desirable. Once the fretter realizes that suppressed feelings are heightening his or her response to minor events, it naturally diffuses some of the charge. Their considerable energy can then be harnessed and sublimated into a Sherlock-style search for what makes them tick!

The Best Treatment for Anxiety Is Involvement

People who get their knickers in a knot over nothing need distractions to carry their concerns out of anxious rumination. Their habits of introspection create a sort of whirlpool, its dizzying momentum of panic sucking them ever downward. Any involvement that can interrupt this reverse osmosis effect will help, because it encourages them to think outside themselves.

For example, people with anxiety or depression, even under medication, may still find elements of their lives largely dissatisfying. Let's face it. Many events and situations are almost impossible to see through rose-colored glasses. There is considerable disappointment, danger, and senselessness out there in the real world. And there is almost always the reminder of people with better, easier lives to exacerbate the angst.

But nothing bridles nervousness like an absorbing activity. The experience of "time flying" is a useful goal here. Interest and confidence in any activity increase with each successive success. They are like vines hanging above a jungle of disquietude. The more of these that can be grasped and used for transport, the more quickly time passes. Fast-passing time has the effect of speeding us toward recovery.

The same shift can occur if people volunteer in new venues, giving of themselves in new ways. Giving has an uncannily rewarding quality. This might be demonstrated through work with a local charity or toward a common political or educational cause. The psychological application is really nothing more than a reminder that "busy hands are happy hands," especially for hands that will otherwise be wringing.

People Who Are Addicted
to Watching Violence
Are Often Suppressing Plenty of It

That's why violence sells! The media knocks us silly with bloodshed, perversion, and suffering and we just keep coming back for more. And if fictional drama is good, bigger-than-life real discord that has nothing to do with us is even better. Just look at how long the O.J. trial held its audience.

Moviegoers, news watchers, and readers are drawn to horror and dispute as though to their own psyches. For good reason. Nothing is as satisfying as watching strangers or fictional characters suffer and triumph while we stay snug and smug. Even as imagined alter egos pit themselves against insurmountable odds, we are thrilled, but unscathed! Though we're glad their lives are not ours, we recognize, usually unconsciously, a glimmer of our own goblins and our own potential within them. That recognition is what makes ratings soar.

Everyone has some conflicts squirreled away in their unconscious. But when individuals become overly agitated or obsessed with events that have no personal bearing on their lives, it may reflect an attempt to resolve inner tension or deflect it onto some external conflict.

Overinvolvement in external conflicts is a way of unconsciously forcing ourselves toward unresolved internal conflicts, of which we may not be aware. It allows pent-up feelings to emerge. These emotions can help us work through more personal issues, if we pay attention to them and work to discover and confront their origins.

Doing Nothing Can Be Very Pushy

Just ask anyone who is close to someone whose policy is "nothing doing." Passive-aggressive types get their own way by being entirely inactive in the middle of activity. Whatever way you turn, there they are, hunkered down into some silent solo sit-in. You entreat them, you try to move beyond them, but the drag from their inertia slows your progress at every turn.

Passive-aggressives don't come on time. They don't leave on time. They don't answer questions (except with more questions). They don't make the first move. They don't make the second move. They just don't.

Passive-aggressives have discovered that doing nothing is a great way to express anger and still keep their nose clean. By being immutable, they can drive others into apoplectic fury. Best of all, to onlookers that fury appears to have little to do with them, because they have *done nothing*.

Dealing with passive-aggressive people is like playing a game of chicken or learning to drive in Italy. Passive-aggressives thwart your progress with feet of clay. When you reposition yourself to compensate for their bullheaded immobility, you are playing into their game. *Cluck, cluck, cluck, cluck*.

My advice is to set your own course, a course that does not depend on them doing anything other than what they do best—nothing. Be as immutable to their influence as they are to yours, and march forward. If passive-aggressives get in your way, don't mention it. Do nothing.

If you yourself excel at passive-aggression, congratulations. But watch out for people who learn to drive in Italy.

Behind Many Spoken Fears
Lurk Unconscious Wishes

Voiced apprehensions are sometimes our best clues about people's unconscious desires. They occasionally relay a suppressed hope that the fear will actually be realized, even when that eventuality wouldn't, on the surface of it, make sense.

"I hope you don't fall down the stairs and break your neck, dear," the wife may say to her bullheaded husband who is ignoring her advice about how much luggage he can carry.

"The company will just fall apart after I retire," remarks the employee who is about to continue to an uncertain future.

"I know you're going to leave me," says an uncommitted lover.

These people may be unconsciously hoping that outside forces will bring a hidden longing to fruition. Sometimes our hopes are all we have. We're law-abiding. We've been taught to toe the line, make no ripples. We're cowards. We're tentative about our choices. We don't want to take responsibility for changing our own lives so we resort to hope. We involuntarily wish that fate will intervene, and we occasionally express this wish.

Not all voiced concerns are laced with cryptic volition. But as with the unsolicited denial, beware when people predict the worst, especially when their prognosis repeats itself with any frequency.

Those Who Bully May Have Been Previously Victimized

Paul Simon wrote, "I'd rather be a hammer than a nail." And who wouldn't? But, the *perception* that being a victim or a bully is an either-or choice is entirely wrong. Believing that one must be either a heavy banger or spindly little pin cultivates and perpetuates hostility, for all parties concerned and, on a broader scale, for society.

Whippin' boys who were the brunt of aggressive parents often "get theirs" as adults. They may have taken it in the teeth from Mom or Dad, and finally got enough chest hairs to unload their accumulated anger onto someone else. That's why we find so many child abusers who were abused themselves as children. But victims are not always children. They come in all ages, and any of them can be reconstituted as a retributive aggressor.

Sadly, the vengeful do not necessarily seek the person who mistreated them for restitution. Victims may pick up the hammer to victimize almost anyone weaker than they. The pitiful recipients then themselves become aggressors. It seems to them that this will make them feel vindicated, but it doesn't. It just initiates more victims into a loop in which they too may eventually go on to bully. This unstoppable and tragic disorder has ramifications everywhere, from familial violence to community violence to ethnic violence.

This is not to say that all bullies were victimized, just sometimes. Nor does it excuse bullies who were abused in childhood from responsibility for their actions, much as defense attorneys would like us to believe otherwise. This principle merely explains the syndrome. Acknowledging the roots that can lead people to knock their way through life oppressing and intimidating may broaden the realization that there are many choices, not just hammers and nails.

Bad People Act, Whereas
Good People Only Fantasize

We are each *capable* of deceit, atrocity, violence, and a whole wretched list of bad stuff. Given bad upbringing, bad exposures, bad influences, bad events, that capability may grow. Few people are entirely exempt from wrongdoing. And even those who do not act criminally are still *capable* of it.

There isn't anything mysterious or mystical about this, though some religions explain it in spiritual terms. We are biologically "wired" for survival and sometimes "survival" can seem to depend on criminal action. This is too simplistic, of course, because complex influences—both external and internal biochemical ones—push people toward violence.

The media tends to stratify our population, clearly demarcating the line between those who offend and those who don't. Offenders are labeled "insane." The rest of us, smug in our inoffensiveness, are "sane." The truth is we are all a little insane. We all harbor feelings that, given the right circumstances and a good handgun, might lead to insane behavior. People who deny this potential may be covering a powder keg's worth of feelings. Accepting the fragility of our mental health is honest and far less dangerous than denial.

NO SPEEDY CONCLUSIONS

Most of What Drives Us Is Very Well Hidden

Even a child can understand why a paraplegic can't run a marathon on foot. Anyone knows why it is impossible to be in Dubuque and Savannah at the same time. Tangible impediments such as these are obvious. But psychological hindrances are not so blatant. Why can't a well-dressed bank executive pee in a public restroom? Why does your daughter refuse to sleep without a nightlight? Why won't a talented thirty-year-old keep a job? The idiosyncrasies that drive and impede human endeavor are almost inscrutable and can take many months and sometimes years to become apparent, whether in therapy or in close relationships.

In many cases, these unseen forces are more potent influences than the concrete variety. They can help us overcome the inadequacies of bodies and time. Or they can tangle the mental circuitry into a continually misfiring mayhem that blocks natural potential and reduces gifted people to numbskulls. Whether prod or encumbrance, our deeply complicated emotional world bears observation. It is critical to scrutinize these invisible powers, and to *value* them.

Valuing them, even if they have been detrimental, gives them voice. And once they are heard, they are better understood. With improved understanding, we can stop stumbling over them. They aren't so much like trip wires in the dark, because the lights have been turned on.

Buzzwords Never Cured Anyone

There is so much information and communication about psychotherapy these days, that the even the most superficial exposure to it is sometimes enough to help the everyman distinguish behaviors as depressive, passive-aggressive, manic-depressive, etc. This knack, in and of itself, is ineffectual, not to mention annoying. First, people who suffer from even incidental emotional problems may not take kindly to labeling. The other glitch is that the ability to identify the behavior doesn't necessarily signify an ability to help treat the behavior. This can take years of training.

There are infinite shades of mental illness, and few emotional tribulations fall neatly into the categories that have become buzzwords. The ease of labeling people overlooks the subtleties that create whole humans and the full range of emotional response. *The person is not the label.* Insanity is within me. It is within you. The mosaic of emotions sometimes presents itself as one of the categories that have become so colloquial (depressive, etc.), but more often combinations of pathologies are at work. Lay people usually don't have the knowledge to get a handle and keep a handle on the intermingling patterns and lead their "patient" through the necessary steps toward recovery. The label is epithet, not diagnosis.

Further, labeling a behavior as "neurotic" ignores the history of the behavior. Say, for example, a partner or coworker's unreasonable demands for compulsive neatness. He or she may have developed that sense of order to keep sane as a child, when the behavior may have been a distraction from a tough situation. Or take the person who is distrusting of authority figures now because they once had real fear of someone powerful. Behaviors that are "crazy" now maybe made perfect sense in a world that no longer exists, the world of childhood.

Labeling stigmatizes the unfortunate victim and tends to suggest the labeler as somehow superior. My experience is that those people who hasten to categorize others are usually those who lack the patience and compassion to help.

If Therapy Isn't Helping,
Get a New Therapist's Input

Life is a roller coaster. Now, imagine that your consciousness is a car on this hair-raising E Ticket ride. The excitement and terror just won't end. With little information, your consciousness is clueless, unprepared for the swift turns and descents that bring your stomach into your throat. Without knowing your unconscious mind, you're a theme park hostage kept in perpetual spin by events that are not always amusing, and often far from it.

People seek therapy because they don't find this fun. They want to anticipate the dips and spins and respond more healthfully. They want control! Therapy cannot promise control over life, but it can teach patients how to manage their emotions and cultivate personal well-being. In short, good therapy stirs the consciousness out of its oblivion. With effective treatment, some part of you should awaken. You should be better prepared for the inevitable vagaries of that roller coaster. When, over a period of time, this feeling of preparedness doesn't grow, it may be time to find another therapist, an eventuality that many patients are reluctant to face. This is understandable since they have already invested greatly, both personally and financially, in the present therapist.

It is not enough to admire your therapist. Some people, especially those who are delusional with low self-esteem, will devalue everything and everyone else before they abandon their commitment to the person with whom they've shared their innermost thoughts, their therapist. This is faulty logic on their part.

Remember, the goal is to feel better. If this does not occur, if you still feel like a clueless roller-coaster detainee, something is wrong. You need help and a different sort of help than you are currently receiving.

In this situation, your present therapist should be open to a consultation with a new therapist. Sometimes, even often, a consultation can rejuvenate his or her therapy with a new approach. If that doesn't work, it may be time to switch or augment with an entirely new therapist. Not all therapists work for all patients.

People Can Overdo Shrink-Think

Psychotherapists can't help it. Our careers are about spotting people's failings, and this ability just naturally spills over into our nonprofessional lives too. Those who train for and practice psychotherapy concentrate all day long on the most downbeat aspects of life imaginable. It sounds negative and it is. People don't seek therapy because they feel good. They come to us with their weaknesses, their unhappiness, and their bottomless dissatisfactions.

Recognizing that these people need help, we are sustained through the negativity by the idea that as medical professionals we can indeed help them. Everything in our experience encourages us to analyze people and interpret their actions according to the time-tested principles summed up in this book. Culling from an immense reservoir of research, we help patients connect to the sources of their malaise, and then look after them until they are able to put their newfound intelligence to work in their lives.

This takes time and patience and time and patience. So just as this book teaches the reader to think like a shrink, I counsel against *acting* as a shrink. My hope is you will be able to identify what could be plausible pathologies more easily. But a quick diagnosis is not the same as a cure. Effective therapy takes time and it takes training.

My advice is, leave the pathology-busting to the professionals who have the tools to lead patients away from their suffering at a healthful pace. *Concentrate instead on positive action and positive views within your own life. This book gives you some of the tools.*

In the final analysis, this book's contents can help illuminate reasons for puzzling behavior and problematic interactions, reasons that may even help you think less judgmentally about those around you. But as I've written elsewhere here, no self-help book can take the place of either the therapeutic relationship or real-life interpersonal relations. There is no substitute for getting out there and resolving your conflicted emotions with people who care for you.

Acceptance Is a Critical Step Toward Emotional Health

Somehow, Americans got the idea that the American dream included the utopia of perpetual *happiness*. When the ideal doesn't occur, they think they're being cheated out of something inalienable. From there, they gravitate to the self-help-book section, join support groups, make a beeline for the shrink, and knock back the antidepressants. Tightening their grip on the goal of their ultimate gratification, they start overhauling everything around them, nearest and dearest first.

The problem is that there is just no telling what will transpire, no tried-and-true formula for *la vie en rose*. Even with the most highfalutin Ph.D.s and spiritual advisors on the task, it is unreasonable to expect that if you do A through L perfectly and those around you can be convinced or coerced into performing M through Z, you will find and keep happiness. In fact, it's not just unreasonable. It's delusional. You may never be happy.

Not only elusive, happiness is ephemeral, coming with life's ups and going with life's downs. In other parts of the world, places with fewer material comforts and less security, expectations are lower . . . sometimes much lower. Recognizing that happiness is fleeting, and that it will never be tied to large goals or Zoloft, people celebrate simple events. In many ways, though their material comforts are more scant, their relationship with themselves and with their loved ones has less internal pressure on it. They save their anxiety for goals that are tied to their physical survival.

Acceptance is one of the biggest messages of this book. By acceptance, I do not mean resignation or abandoning your personal growth. Rather, acceptance means stop fixating on problems that, though they may have solutions, cannot be solved by you. Let go! If your objective were emotional health, instead of happiness, you would let go immediately. Why make yourself crazy?

With an attitude of *acceptance,* most people can augment their lives with additional relationships and activities that provide what their existing emotional worlds cannot. They may still feel a void, but lack of fulfillment will drive them to grow. And growth is good.

GLOSSARY

The following comprise only those definitions of a word applicable to psychology.

affect—The observed expression of feeling. Appropriate or inappropriate; full range of feeling or blunted.

anal—Psychosexual development's second stage during which gratification is derived from the ability to expulse or retain feces.

anal character—Personality traits including exactness, compulsivity, and rigidity, associated with preoccupation with the anal phase as a child, with effects lingering into adulthood; manifested in fastidious, very detail oriented, and parsimonious behavior.

antisocial—A pattern of behavior in which the rights of others are persistently violated.

bipolar disorder—Characterized by two extremes, a psychological disorder wherein periods of mania alternate with periods of depression, usually interspersed with relatively long intervals of even mood; also called manic-depressive illness.

conscious—The part of the mind comprising psychic material of which the individual is aware; the material one knows.

consciousness—The state of being aware of one's own existence, sensations, thoughts, surroundings, etc.

cortex—The cerebral cortex, the outer layer of the brain associated with voluntary action, learning, memory, and expressions of individuality.

counterintuitive—The opposite of what one would naturally expect to occur.

counterphobic—Deliberately looking for and confronting a situation one fears in an attempt to overcome the fear.

drive theory—Philosophical premise that people are impelled by inner sexual and/or aggressive desires of a primal nature.

egocentric—Self-centered and having little or no regard for interests, beliefs, or attitudes other than one's own.

egotist—A vain, boastful, selfish person.

Electra complex—Unconscious libidinous desire of a daughter for her father that remains unresolved, based on the Greek myth of Electra and Agamemnon.

extrovert—An outgoing person who is preoccupied with external involvements.

frontal lobe—That anterior part of each cerebral hemisphere, in front of the central sulcus, occupied with planning, judgment, reasoning, and other strategic thinking.

introvert—A person who is preoccupied with his or her own thoughts.

issues—Shrink-speak for emotionally powerful problem areas.

limbic system—The seat of the emotions, occupying a ring of interconnected structures in the midline of the brain around the hypothalamus, involved with memory.

manic-depressive illness—An affective disorder characterized by periods of mania alternating with periods of depression, usually interspersed with relatively long intervals of even mood; also called bipolar disorder.

masochism—The condition in which gratification, sexual or otherwise, depends on incurring suffering, physical pain, and humiliation.

masochist—A person who seems to find pleasure in pain or to seek pain, whether self-inflicted or inflicted by others.

meds—Medicine.

narcissism—Love of oneself; erotic gratification derived from admiration of one's own physical or mental attributes. Narcissism is a normal condition at the infantile level of personality development. Some narcissism is necessary for survival; excessive narcissism is pathological.

narcissist—An excessively vain and self-absorbed person.

neurosis—An emotional problem that dominates the personality; a functional disorder that includes feelings of anxiety, obsessive thoughts, compulsive acts, and physical complaints without objective evidence of disease, in various degrees and patterns; also, a relatively mild personality disorder typified by excessive indecision or worry and a degree of social maladjustment; an unusual condition of misery determined by unconscious conflicts.

neurotic—Of or pertaining to neurosis; also, a person who suffers from emotional problems.

object relations—A pattern of behavior in response to others, established in early life in response to family, that continues throughout life.

obsessive-compulsive disorder—A neurosis characterized by persistent intrusion of unwanted thoughts which become obsessions, or the performance of actions, such as repeated hand washing, that one is unable to prevent.

obsessive-compulsive personality—A personality style characterized by rigidity, obstinancy, detail-orientation, and the need for control.

Oedipus complex—The unresolved, unconscious libidinous desire of a son for his mother, based on the Greek myth of Oedipus and Jocasta wherein Oedipus unknowingly kills his father and marries his mom and is subsequently overwhelmed with guilt when he finds out; these events are emotional rather than actual in psychological principle.

oral—The earliest phase of psychosexual development, lasting from birth to one year of age or longer, during which gratification is obtained from eating, sucking, and biting; also, the sublimation of feelings experienced during the oral stage of childhood; additionally, gratification by stimulation of the lips or membranes of the mouth, as in sucking, eating, or talking.

panic attack—An intense attack of anxiety characterized by feelings of impending doom, with trembling, sweating, pounding heart, and other physical symptoms that seem to come out of nowhere.

paranoia—A mental disorder characterized by uncontrolled delusions and the projection of personal conflicts onto others, which are ascribed to their supposed hostility, sometimes progressing to disturbed consciousness, and aggressive acts that the paranoid performs believing they are in self-defense or as a mission; alternatively, excessive suspicion of the motives of others; a state wherein one is unduly suspicious.

paranoid—A person suffering from paranoia.

passive-aggressive personality—A personality disorder characterized by aggressive behavior expressed in passive ways, such as procrastination, obstinacy, or sulking.

pathology—Any deviation from a healthy, normal, or efficient condition; alternatively, the science or the study of the origin, nature, and course of diseases.

personality—The sum of the physical, mental, emotional, and social characteristics of an individual, or the organized pattern of behavioral characteristics of the individual; literally, the voice *(son)* that speaks from the mask *(pers)*.

psychiatrist—A professional who practices psychiatry.

psychiatry—The practice or science of diagnosing and treating mental disorders that demands a medical degree to understand organic dosages; the practice includes medications.

psychic—Pertaining to or noting mental phenomena.

psychoanalysis—A technical procedure for investigating unconscious mental processes and for treating psychoneuroses.

psychologist—A professional who practices psychology, focusing on the psyche, not medications.

psychology—The science of the mind or of mental states and processes, as well as behavior.

psychoneurosis—Neurosis.

psychopathy—A mental disorder in which an individual manifests amoral and antisocial behavior, an inability to love or establish meaningful personal relationships, extreme egocentricity, a failure to learn from experience, etc.

psychopath—A person who suffers from psychopathy.

psychopharmaceuticals—Psychoactive drugs that have a profound or significant effect on mental processes.

psychosexual—Pertaining to the relationship of psychological and sexual phenomena.

psychosis—A mental disorder characterized by symptoms such as delusions or hallucinations, which indicate impaired contact with reality.

sadism—Gratification gained through causing pain or degradation to others.

sociopath—A person whose behavior is antisocial and who lacks a sense of moral responsibility and social conscience.

transference—The shift of emotions, particularly those experienced during childhood, from one person "there and then" to another person "here and now."

unconscious—The part of the mind containing psychic material that is only rarely accessible to awareness but nevertheless has a profound influence on behavior.

SELECTED BIBLIOGRAPHY

This book is not just a reflection of my thinking, but also a distillation of often-mainstream opinion in a field often rife with controversy. It has been greatly enriched by books, as well as conversations, with my esteemed colleagues, the most outstanding of which follow:

Benedek, Elissa P. *How to Help Your Child Overcome Your Divorce* (Washington, D.C.: American Psychiatric Press, 1995). This book is a practical resource for many of the issues that divorce creates.

Burns, David. *The Feeling Good Handbook* (New York: Plume, 1999). If you want a book that makes cognitive therapy understandable and usable, this is it.

Colarusso, Calvin A., and Robert Nemiroff. *Adult Development* (New York: Plenum Press, 1981).

Colarusso, Calvin A. *Child and Adult Development* (New York: Plenum Press, 1992); *Fulfillment in Adulthood* (New York: Plenum Press, 1994). All of Colarusso's works provide sophisticated information in an easy-to-assimilate language and format. In my judgment, they are essential reading to the practice of psychotherapy that simply does not exist as accessibly elsewhere.

DSM-IV, (Washington, D.C.: American Psychiatric Press, 1994). This book is considered the "bible" of psychiatric diagnosis.

Gabbard, Glen O. *Psychodynamic Psychiatry in Clinical Practice* (Washington, D.C.: American Psychiatric Press, 1994). This book has become, and will remain, a classic. There is simply no other synthesis of psychoanalytic theory that is as comprehensive, well written, and authoritative.

Gay, Peter. *Freud: A Life for Our Time* (New York: W.W. Norton and Company, 1988). This biography teaches more about the human mind than anything available in pop psychology or even in the DSM-IV (see above), for that matter.

Gottman, John. *Raising an Emotionally Intelligent Child* (New York: Simon & Schuster, 1997). This is one of the most scientifically grounded guides for the lay person.

Millon, Theodore, with Roger D. Davis. *Disorders of Personality: DSM-IV and Beyond* (New York: John Wiley and Sons, 1996). Though clearly not for the lay reader, it provides the most scientifically rigorous elucidation of modern personality theory. The summaries of past history and current ideas are invaluable and accessible.

Nicholi, Armand H. *The Harvard Guide to Psychiatry,* 3rd ed. (Cambridge, Mass.: Harvard University Press, 1999). For an overview of the field, this is a terrific updated resource.

Ursano, Robert J., Steven M. Sonnenberg, and Susan G. Lazar. *Psychodynamic Psychotherapy.* (Washington, D.C.: American Psychiatric Press, 1991).

Weiner, Jerry M. *Textbook of Child and Adolescent Psychiatry.* (Washington, D.C.: American Psychiatric Press, 1997). Weiner's is an informative read for parents and educators.